COOK'S COLLECTION

FAST & SIMPLE

Fuss-free and tasty recipe ideas
for the modern cook

LOVE FOOD™

CONTENTS

INTRODUCTION

Fast cooking is all about using fresh, vibrant ingredients and cooking them quickly and simply. You can forget uninspiring quick fixes and the same old favourites, recycled again and again – this book opens the door to a world of exciting flavours and speedy cooking techniques, cutting the amount of time you spend in the kitchen while producing amazingly tasty meals.

We all seem to have less time these days, and cooking often takes second place to all the other demands of our busy schedules. The temptation can be to reach for take-away meals or ready-made dinners, but these come with obvious disadvantages. For one thing, they're often pricey, and for another they're not particularly healthy. But help is at hand! *Fast & Simple* is *the* cookbook for busy people. With over 100 fuss-free recipes that can be prepared and cooked in 45 minutes or less, you can have a delicious meal on the table in a flash.

Preparation is essential for speedy cooking but whether it's a busy job, the familiar stretch of family life, or a jam-packed weekend, sometimes finding the time each evening to think about mealtimes can be a challenge. And that's where a little forward planning at the beginning of each week can come in handy. If you're able to think about the week ahead, plan what you're going to cook on each night this will save time.

With your meals for the week in mind make a shopping list of ingredients you'll need for each dish; you can either go for an old-fashioned list pinned to the fridge or use one of the many tablet or smartphone apps that are designed to help you manage your shopping lists. These apps allow you to create lists, scan barcodes, sync your lists on multiple devices and even send notifications to other family members to pick up ingredients on their way home. With your meal plan and shopping list in hand, you can do one quick trip to get everything you need – or for an even quicker shop, make use of online supermarket apps. They make light work of grocery shopping, remembering favourite or recently purchased items and will deliver to you.

A weekly shop of the items that you need will ensure you have a well-stocked storecupboard – which is essential for the speedy cook. There's a huge range of convenient long-life ingredients that are useful to have on standby to use in your cooking – dried pasta, rice, couscous, quinoa, curry paste, pesto, tahini, miso, tomatoes, sweetcorn and beans, ready-roasted peppers; the list is endless. Keep a running check of what you have and add to your shopping list as you go along.

As well as stocking up on ingredients, it's a good idea to do a little prep for the next day, if you have time. Wash and trim veggies, dice meats, whip up a marinade and put your meat for the next day in it straight away, or whisk together a big jar of vinaigrette for the week's salads. If you know you'll need an onion for two meals in a row, chop two and keep one in a polythene bag for the following night's dinner. Likewise, herbs can be finely chopped and frozen, with a bit of olive oil or water, in small portions in an ice cube tray. Later you can toss them into sauces, soups or stir-fries for a burst of fresh flavour. The freezer is also useful for freezing cooked food – save time by cooking double portions of foods that store well and freezing half for another time.

Freshness is absolutely essential – quick-cook dishes benefit from produce that is in peak condition. The freezer is great for keeping a supply of meat, fish and veggies to hand, but do make sure you always allow enough time for thawing – take meat, fish etc. out of the freezer the night before and leave it in the fridge overnight.

Some kitchen equipment is particularly useful when you're cooking quick meals – you'll find that your grill really comes into its own, and a wok for stir-fries, a griddle pan and a selection of baking sheets and trays are essential. Don't be afraid to pull out the food processor, even for jobs that seem small, especially if you have a dishwasher. Slicing vegetables, grating cheese, mixing together sauces, marinades and salad dressing is light work for these useful devices – and they won't take long to clean afterwards.

To ensure complete success read through the recipe carefully and line up all the ingredients, pots and pans and other equipment that you'll need before you start cooking. Boil the kettle if you're cooking pasta and keep your scissors handy for snipping herbs, cutting sheets of pastry and trimming meat. The five minutes you spend organizing yourself will pay big time dividends later on. Multi-tasking is key to maximise your time when quick-cooking. Getting longer cooking ingredients in the oven while you make a quick salad will ensure you get fast results.

With this 'quick-cooking' mindset mastered, any meal of the day will become a breeze, and an exciting array of recipes awaits you. You can make a delicious breakfast muesli, porridge or smoothie in 10–15 minutes. For lunch, feel virtuous with the Green Goddess Salad (see page 88). For dinner, Mixed Bean, Nut & Kale Stew (see page 118) is nutritious as well as comforting. And you can get your indulgent chocolate fix with a cake: Hot Chocolate Fudge Layer Cake (see page 188) – from start to finish in 30 minutes!

And, in the end, you'll not only have a quick meal but a totally delicious one too, as lightly cooked vegetables retain their freshness, crunch, colour and flavour – and grilling or griddling quickly seals in the juicy goodness of meat. So, what are you waiting for? Get cooking!

CHAPTER ONE

BREAKFAST

HEALTHIEST-EVER MUESLI

SERVES: *4* | **PREP:** *10 mins* | **COOK:** *No cooking*

INGREDIENTS

150 g/5½ oz oat flakes

100 g/3½ oz rye flakes

40 g/1½ oz walnuts

40 g/1½ oz Brazil nuts

10 g/¼ oz sunflower seeds

10 g/¼ oz pumpkin seeds

15 g/½ oz raisins

*15 g/½ oz ready-to-eat dried
   apricots, chopped*

2 tbsp milled linseeds

1. In a mixing bowl, thoroughly combine the oat flakes and rye flakes.

2. Chop the walnuts and Brazil nuts and add to the flakes with the sunflower seeds, pumpkin seeds and raisins.

3. Mix the dried apricots with the milled linseeds – the seed meal will coat the apricots and prevent them sticking together. Stir the mixture into the muesli.

4. Store in an airtight container if not using immediately. You can easily double or treble the quantity and store in the refrigerator for up to 1 week.

SPICED QUINOA PORRIDGE WITH BERRIES

SERVES: *4* | **PREP:** *5 mins* | **COOK:** *15 mins*

INGREDIENTS

100 g/3½ oz quinoa flakes
1 tbsp milled linseeds
½ tsp sea salt
½ tsp ground cinnamon
¼ tsp ground ginger
¼ tsp ground nutmeg
550 ml/19 fl oz almond milk
1 tbsp agave nectar
2 tbsp golden berries
3 tbsp desiccated coconut flakes
40 g/1½ oz fresh blueberries
40 g/1½ oz fresh raspberries
40 g/1½ oz fresh blackberries

1. In a large bowl, combine the quinoa flakes, linseeds, salt and spices.

2. Heat the almond milk in a saucepan and add the quinoa flake mixture. Stir and bring to a simmer, then add the agave nectar. Cook, stirring frequently, for about 6 minutes, or until you have a fairly thick porridge and the flakes are soft. Add a little extra milk or water, if you prefer a thinner porridge, and stir well.

3. Ladle the porridge into serving bowls and top each with a quarter of the golden berries, coconut flakes and fresh berries. Serve immediately.

CARAMEL PECAN APPLES

SERVES: *4* | **PREP:** *10–15 mins* | **COOK:** *10 mins*

INGREDIENTS

55 g/2 oz unsalted butter

55 g/2 oz light muscovado sugar

4 crisp eating apples, cored and cut into wedges

1 tsp ground cinnamon

4 thick slices of brioche

4 tbsp rum or apple juice

25 g/1 oz pecan nuts

1. Melt the butter in a frying pan, add the sugar, apples and cinnamon and stir. Cook over a medium heat, stirring occasionally, for 5–6 minutes until caramelized and golden.

2. Meanwhile, toast the brioche on both sides until golden.

3. Stir the rum and pecan nuts into the pan and cook for a further 1 minute.

4. Transfer the toasted brioche to warmed serving plates. Spoon the apple mixture over and serve immediately.

PEAR & HAZELNUT PANCAKES

SERVES: *4* | **PREP:** *20 mins* | **COOK:** *10 mins*

INGREDIENTS

*200 g/7 oz chocolate hazelnut
    spread*
8 ready-made pancakes
4 ripe pears
40 g/1½ oz unsalted butter, melted
2 tbsp demerara sugar
*55 g/2 oz toasted chopped
    hazelnuts, to serve*

1. Preheat the grill to high. Gently heat the chocolate spread in a small saucepan until soft.

2. Using a palette knife, spread each pancake with a little of the warmed chocolate spread.

3. Peel, core and chop the pears. Arrange the pears over the chocolate spread, then bring the opposite sides of the pancakes over the filling to enclose it.

4. Lightly brush an ovenproof dish with a little of the melted butter.

5. Arrange the pancakes in the dish. Brush the pancakes with the remaining melted butter and sprinkle with the demerara sugar.

6. Place the dish under the preheated grill and cook for 4–5 minutes, until bubbling and lightly browned.

7. Scatter the toasted hazelnuts over the pancakes and serve hot.

STRAWBERRY & PASSION FRUIT YOGURTS

SERVES: *4* | **PREP:** *20–25 mins, plus chilling* | **COOK:** *2–3 mins*

INGREDIENTS

20 g/¾ oz desiccated coconut
200 g/7 oz strawberries, hulled
juice and finely grated zest of 1 lime
350 g/12 oz Greek-style natural
* yogurt*
4 tsp clear honey
2 passion fruit, halved
1 tbsp dried goji berries, roughly
* chopped*

1. Add the coconut to a dry frying pan and cook over a medium heat, shaking the pan, for 2–3 minutes until light golden in colour. Remove from the heat and leave to cool.

2. Coarsely mash the strawberries and mix with half the lime juice.

3. Add the lime zest, remaining lime juice, the yogurt and honey to a bowl and stir together. Add three quarters of the cooled coconut to the yogurt, then scoop the seeds from the passion fruit over the top and lightly fold into the yogurt.

4. Layer alternate spoonfuls of strawberry and yogurt in four 200-ml/7-fl oz preserving jars, then sprinkle with the remaining coconut and the goji berries. Clip down the lids and chill until ready to serve. Eat within 24 hours.

HEALTHY FRUIT
& NUT BOWL

SERVES: *4* | **PREP:** *15 mins, plus standing & chilling* | **COOK:** *No cooking*

INGREDIENTS

1 orange

*2 mangoes, peeled, stoned and
    chopped*

4 tbsp chia seeds

4–5 tbsp milk

2 tbsp goji berries

seeds from 2 passion fruits

55 g/2 oz pineapple, cut into chunks

2 tbsp sunflower seeds

2 tbsp pumpkin seeds

55 g/2 oz redcurrants

2 kiwi fruits, peeled and sliced

2 tbsp flaked almonds, toasted

1. Grate the orange rind, then peel the orange and put the flesh into a food processor with the chopped mango. Process for a few seconds to break everything down.

2. Add the orange rind, chia seeds and milk and process again for 20–30 seconds, scraping down any mixture from the side of the bowl. Leave to stand for 5 minutes.

3. Process the mixture again, then divide it between four bowls and chill in the refrigerator for 10 minutes.

4. Top with the remaining ingredients and serve.

CINNAMON &
RAISIN SPIRALS

MAKES: *12 spirals* | **PREP:** *15 mins* | **COOK:** *15 mins*

INGREDIENTS

*1 x 325-g/11½-oz sheet ready-rolled
   puff pastry*
25 g/1 oz butter, softened
2 tbsp caster sugar
1 tsp ground cinnamon
55 g/2 oz raisins
2 tbsp apricot jam

1. Preheat the oven to 220°C/425°F/Gas Mark 7. Dampen two baking sheets with a sprinkling of cold water. Unroll the pastry and spread with the butter, leaving a 1-cm/½-inch border. Mix together the sugar and cinnamon, and sprinkle evenly over the butter, then scatter over the raisins.

2. Gently roll up the pastry from one long side. Using a sharp knife, cut through the roll to make 12 even-sized rounds. Place the rounds flat side down on the prepared baking sheets. Use the palm of your hand to flatten out each round slightly. Bake in the preheated oven for 12–15 minutes, or until risen and golden.

3. Transfer the pastries to a wire rack. Meanwhile, put the jam into a small saucepan and heat over a low heat until warm, then strain through a fine sieve into a small bowl to make a smooth glaze. Quickly brush the glaze over the hot pastries. Serve warm or cold.

BEETROOT & POMEGRANATE SMOOTHIE BOWL

SERVES: *1* | **PREP:** *10 mins, plus optional chilling* | **COOK:** *No cooking*

INGREDIENTS

1 large beetroot, peeled and
    chopped
15 g/½ oz spinach leaves
3 tbsp pomegranate seeds
100 ml/3½ fl oz water
juice of 1 orange
1 tbsp clear honey
125 g/4½ oz natural yogurt
1 tsp wheatgrass powder
2 tsp buckwheat groats
2 round orange slices, halved

1. Put the beetroot in a blender with the spinach, 2 tablespoons of the pomegranate seeds and half the water. Blend until smooth.

2. Add the remaining water, the orange juice, honey, 100 g/3½ oz of the yogurt and the wheatgrass powder to the blender. Blend again.

3. Pour the smoothie into a serving bowl and chill for 1 hour if you have time.

4. Drizzle the remaining yogurt over the smoothie. Sprinkle over the groats and decorate with the orange slices and remaining seeds.

RASPBERRY REJUVENATOR

INGREDIENTS

25 g/1 oz goji berries
1 small banana, peeled and roughly
*   chopped*
115 g/4 oz raspberries
juice of 2 oranges
small handful of crushed ice
*   (optional)*
chilled water, to taste

1. Put the goji berries in a blender and whizz until finely ground.

2. Add the banana, raspberries and orange juice and blend until smooth. Add the crushed ice, if using, and blend again until smooth.

3. Add water to taste, pour into a glass and serve immediately.

SUPER GREENS SMOOTHIE

SERVES: *1* | **PREP:** *15–20 mins* | **COOK:** *No cooking*

INGREDIENTS

1 pear, halved

40 g/1½ oz young spinach

4 fresh flat-leaf parsley sprigs

¼ cucumber, roughly chopped

*½ avocado, stoned, flesh
    scooped out*

½ tsp spirulina powder

chilled water, to taste

1 Brazil nut, roughly chopped

1. Feed the pear through a juicer. Pour the juice into a blender, add the spinach, parsley, cucumber and avocado and blend until smooth. Pour into a glass.

2. Mix the spirulina powder with just enough water to make a thick liquid, then swirl into the juice.

3. Sprinkle over the chopped nut and serve.

BEE POLLEN &
NECTARINE SOOTHER

SERVES: *2* | **PREP:** *15 mins* | **COOK:** *No cooking*

INGREDIENTS

*2 ripe nectarines, stoned and
    quartered*
200 ml/7 fl oz semi-skimmed milk
2 tbsp Greek-style natural yogurt
1 tbsp bee pollen
1 tsp clear honey
handful of ice cubes
1 tsp bee pollen, to decorate
2 nectarine slices, to decorate

1. Place the nectarines, milk, yogurt, bee pollen and honey in a blender and blend until smooth.

2. Add the ice cubes and blend again until completely combined.

3. Pour into chilled glasses and decorate each serving with the bee pollen and a slice of nectarine. Serve immediately.

BLUEBERRY SCONES

MAKES: *8 scones* | **PREP:** *20 mins, plus cooling* | **COOK:** *20 mins*

INGREDIENTS

250 g/9 oz plain flour, plus extra
   for dusting
2 tsp baking powder
¼ tsp salt
85 g/3 oz butter, chilled and diced,
   plus extra for greasing and
   to serve
70 g/2½ oz golden caster sugar
115 g/4 oz blueberries
1 egg
100 ml/3½ fl oz buttermilk
1 tbsp milk
1 tbsp demerara sugar

1. Preheat the oven to 200°C/400°F/Gas Mark 6. Lightly grease a large baking sheet.

2. Sift together the flour, baking powder and salt into a large bowl, and stir in the butter. Rub the butter into the flour until the mixture resembles fine breadcrumbs. Stir in the caster sugar and blueberries.

3. Beat together the egg and buttermilk and pour into the bowl. Mix to a soft dough. Turn out the dough onto a floured work surface and knead gently.

4. Shape and gently pat the dough into an 18-cm/7-inch round. Use a sharp knife to cut into eight even-sized wedges. Place the wedges on the prepared baking sheet. Brush the tops of the scones with the milk and sprinkle over the demerara sugar. Bake in the preheated oven for 20 minutes, or until risen and golden brown. Transfer to a wire rack and leave to cool slightly, then serve with butter.

SUPERFOOD
BREAKFAST BARS

SERVES: *12* | **PREP:** *10 mins, plus cooling* | **COOK:** *20–25 mins*

INGREDIENTS

butter, for greasing

100 g/3½ oz coconut oil

90 g/3¼ oz black treacle

20 g/¾ oz dark muscovado sugar

25 g/1 oz agave syrup

235 g/8½ oz rolled oats

50 g/1¾ oz pecan nuts, roughly chopped

50 g/1¾ oz cocoa nibs

50 g/1¾ oz blueberries

1. Preheat the oven to 180°C/350°F/Gas Mark 4. Grease an 18-cm/7-inch square traybake tin.

2. Put the coconut oil, treacle, sugar and agave syrup into a large saucepan and heat until melted. Stir until the sugar has dissolved, then remove from the heat.

3. Stir in the remaining ingredients and mix well. Pour into the prepared tin and level the top.

4. Bake in the preheated oven for 18–20 minutes, then leave to cool in the tin for 5 minutes before cutting into squares.

5. Leave in the tin to cool completely. Store in an airtight container for up to 5 days.

EGGS BAKED
IN AVOCADOS

SERVES: *4* | **PREP:** *20 mins* | **COOK:** *20 mins*

INGREDIENTS

5 streaky bacon rashers

2 large ripe avocados

4 small eggs

pepper (optional)

hot toast or salsa, to serve
  (optional)

1. Preheat the oven to 220°C/425°F/Gas Mark 7 and the grill to high. Cook the bacon under the preheated grill for 5–6 minutes until crisp, then roughly chop.

2. Halve and stone the avocados. Scoop out enough flesh to make a hole big enough to hold an egg. Place cut side up in a bun tin or muffin tin – the holes will prevent them tilting over.

3. Drop 3–4 pieces of bacon into the base of each avocado. Crack an egg into a cup. To make sure the egg doesn't slide out of the avocado when you pour it in, scoop out the egg yolk with a spoon and drop it into the hole, then lightly whisk the egg white with a fork to break it up and pour in enough to fill up the hole.

4. Repeat with the remaining eggs and season to taste with pepper, if using. Bake in the preheated oven for 15 minutes until the whites of the eggs are just set. Sprinkle with the remaining bacon and serve immediately with hot toast, or salsa, if using.

EGG-WHITE OMELETTE

INGREDIENTS

¼ red pepper, deseeded

2 large egg whites

1 spring onion, thinly sliced

pinch of salt

pinch of pepper

1 spray of vegetable oil or olive
*   oil spray*

25 g/1 oz fresh goat's cheese

2 tsp chopped fresh basil, plus extra
*   sprigs to garnish*

1 tbsp snipped fresh chives,
*   to garnish*

1. Preheat the grill. Put the red pepper skin side up on a baking tray and cook under the preheated grill until it begins to blacken. Remove and place in a polythene bag or a bowl covered with clingfilm and set aside until cool enough to handle. Peel off and discard the blackened skin and dice the flesh.

2. In a small bowl, mix the egg whites, spring onion, salt and pepper together, stirring to combine well.

3. Coat a frying pan with the oil spray and heat over a medium heat. Add the egg mixture and cook for about 3 minutes, or until the egg is set, turning the pan frequently and running a palette knife around the edge to maintain a thin, even layer of egg.

4. Crumble the goat's cheese in a strip down the centre of the omelette, then top with the diced pepper and the basil. Fold the sides over the filling and slide the omelette onto a plate. Serve immediately, garnished with basil and chives.

SAVOURY OATMEAL WITH HOT SMOKED SALMON & AVOCADO

SERVES: *4* | **PREP:** *10 mins* | **COOK:** *12-15 mins*

INGREDIENTS

150 g/5½ oz rolled oats
350 ml/12 fl oz milk
600 ml/1 pint water
4 eggs
4 tsp creamed horseradish
200 g/7 oz hot smoked salmon,
 flaked
2 avocados, stoned, peeled and
 sliced
pepper (optional)
2 tbsp pumpkin seeds, to garnish

1. Place the oats in a saucepan with the milk and water. Bring to the boil over a medium heat, then reduce the heat and simmer for 4–5 minutes until thick and creamy.

2. Meanwhile, poach the eggs in a saucepan of gently simmering water for 4–5 minutes.

3. Mix the creamed horseradish with half the smoked salmon and stir into the porridge.

4. Divide the porridge between four warmed bowls and top each one with some avocado slices, a poached egg and some of the remaining salmon. Season to taste with pepper, if using.

5. Toast the pumpkin seeds in a dry frying pan, sprinkle over the porridge and serve.

EGG TORTILLA WITH FETA & SWEETCORN

SERVES: *4* | **PREP:** *15 mins* | **COOK:** *20 mins*

INGREDIENTS

350 g/12 oz potatoes, cubed

2 tbsp olive oil

1 onion, chopped

1 courgette, coarsely grated

200 g/7 oz canned sweetcorn,
*   drained*

6 eggs

100 g/3½ oz feta cheese, crumbled

salt and pepper (optional)

paprika, to garnish

1. Add a little salt, if using, to a large saucepan of water and bring to the boil. Add the potatoes, bring back to the boil and cook for 5 minutes, or until just tender. Drain well.

2. Heat the oil in a large ovenproof frying pan over a medium heat. Add the onion and cook for 5 minutes, stirring occasionally, until soft. Add the courgette and potatoes and cook for 2 minutes. Stir in the sweetcorn.

3. Preheat the grill to high. Place the eggs in a bowl. Season to taste with salt and pepper, if using, and lightly whisk together. Pour the egg over the vegetables, then sprinkle over the feta cheese and leave to cook for 4–5 minutes, or until almost set.

4. Cook under the preheated grill for 2–3 minutes until bubbling and golden brown. Transfer to a wooden board or warmed serving plates. Garnish with paprika and serve hot or cold.

BAKED MUSHROOMS
WITH HERBED RICOTTA

INGREDIENTS

4 large, flat mushrooms

1 tbsp olive oil

1 shallot, roughly chopped

25 g/1 oz fresh flat-leaf parsley

1 tbsp snipped fresh chives

140 g/5 oz ricotta cheese

salt and pepper (optional)

1. Preheat the oven to 200°C/400°F/Gas Mark 6. Remove the stalks from the mushrooms and set aside. Place the mushrooms in a shallow baking dish and brush with the oil.

2. Put the mushroom stalks, shallot, parsley and chives in a food processor and process until finely chopped. Season to taste with salt and pepper, if using.

3. Place the chopped ingredients in a large bowl with the cheese and stir to mix evenly.

4. Spoon the herbed cheese on top of the mushrooms. Bake in the preheated oven for 15–20 minutes, or until tender and bubbling. Serve immediately.

AVOCADO, BACON & CHILLI FRITTATA

SERVES: *4* | **PREP:** *15 mins* | **COOK:** *15 mins*

INGREDIENTS

1 tbsp vegetable oil

8 streaky bacon rashers, roughly chopped

6 eggs, beaten

3 tbsp double cream

2 large avocados, peeled and sliced

1 red chilli, deseeded and thinly sliced

½ lime

sea salt and pepper (optional)

1. Preheat the grill to medium. Heat the oil in a 20-cm/8-inch ovenproof frying pan over a medium heat. Add the bacon and fry, stirring, for 4–5 minutes, or until crisp and golden. Using a slotted spoon, transfer to a plate lined with kitchen paper. Remove the pan from the heat.

2. Pour the eggs into a bowl, add the cream and season with salt and pepper, if using, then beat. Return the pan to the heat. When it is hot, pour in the egg mixture and cook for 1–2 minutes, without stirring. Sprinkle the bacon and avocado on top and cook for a further 2–3 minutes, or until the frittata is almost set and the underside is golden brown.

3. Place the frittata under the preheated grill and cook for 3–4 minutes, or until the top is golden brown and the egg is set. Scatter with the chilli and squeeze over the lime juice. Cut into wedges and serve immediately.

CHEESY SWEETCORN FRITTERS

SERVES: *8* | **PREP:** *15 mins* | **COOK:** *3–4 mins*

INGREDIENTS

1 egg

200 ml/7 fl oz milk

100 g/3½ oz plain flour

½ tsp baking powder

85 g/3 oz canned sweetcorn kernels,
*   drained*

4 tbsp grated Cheddar cheese

1 tsp snipped fresh chives

2 tsp sunflower oil

1. Put the egg and milk into a medium bowl and beat with a fork.

2. Add the flour and baking powder and beat until smooth. Stir in the sweetcorn, cheese and chives.

3. Heat the oil in a non-stick frying pan over a medium heat. Drop tablespoons of the batter into the pan.

4. Cook for 1–2 minutes until the fritters are puffed up and golden. Turn and cook for a further 1 minute. Remove from the pan, drain on kitchen paper and serve.

CHAPTER TWO

SIDES & SNACKS

QUINOA SALAD WITH FENNEL & ORANGE

SERVES: *4* | **PREP:** *10–15 mins* | **COOK:** *20–25 mins*

INGREDIENTS

850 ml/1½ pints vegetable stock
225 g/8 oz quinoa, rinsed and
*   drained*
3 oranges
250 g/9 oz fennel bulbs, thinly sliced
*   using a mandolin, green fronds*
*   reserved and torn into small*
*   pieces*
2 spring onions, finely chopped
15 g/½ oz fresh flat-leaf parsley,
*   roughly chopped*

DRESSING

juice of ½ lemon
3 tbsp olive oil
pepper (optional)

1. Bring the stock to the boil in a saucepan, add the quinoa and simmer for 10–12 minutes, or until the germs separate from the seeds. Drain off the stock and discard, then spoon the quinoa into a salad bowl and leave to cool.

2. Grate the rind from two of the oranges and put it in a jam jar. Cut a slice off the top and bottom of each of the three oranges, then remove the peel in thin vertical slices and discard. Cut between the membranes, remove and reserve the orange segments, then squeeze the juice from the membranes into the jam jar.

3. Add the reserved orange segments, fennel slices, spring onions and parsley to the quinoa.

4. To make the dressing, add the lemon juice and oil to the jam jar, season to taste with pepper, if using, screw on the lid and shake well. Drizzle over the salad and toss together. Garnish with the fennel fronds and serve immediately.

GAZPACHO SALAD

SERVES: *4* | **PREP:** *10–15 mins* | **COOK:** *No cooking*

INGREDIENTS

500 g/1 lb 2 oz tomatoes, halved, deseeded and diced

85 g/3 oz cucumber, quartered lengthways, deseeded and thickly sliced

1 celery stick, diced

1 spring onion, finely chopped

½ yellow pepper, deseeded and diced

1 tbsp fresh basil leaves, to garnish

DRESSING

40 g/1½ oz sun-dried tomatoes in oil, drained

2 tbsp olive oil

1 tbsp hemp oil

2 tbsp red wine vinegar

1 garlic clove, finely chopped

¼ tsp dried crushed red chillies

pepper (optional)

1. Put the tomatoes, cucumber, celery and spring onion in a salad bowl, then add the yellow pepper and gently toss together.

2. To make the dressing, put the sun-dried tomatoes in a blender. Add the olive oil, hemp oils, vinegar, garlic and chillies. Season to taste with pepper, if using, then process to a coarse paste.

3. Spoon the dressing over the salad, gently toss together, then garnish with the basil leaves.

WARM SLICED BEEF
TABBOULEH SALAD

SERVES: *4* | **PREP:** *15 mins* | **COOK:** *10 mins, plus standing*

INGREDIENTS

100 g/3½ oz bulgar wheat

400 g/14 oz lean beef fillet

200 g/7 oz fresh flat-leaf parsley,
*   finely chopped*

140 g/5 oz fresh mint, finely
*   chopped*

1 red onion, thinly sliced

2 tomatoes, diced

1 tbsp extra virgin olive oil, plus
*   extra for brushing*

juice of 2 lemons

salt and pepper (optional)

1. Place the bulgar wheat in a bowl and pour over boiling water to cover. Leave to soak for 10 minutes. Drain thoroughly, pressing out any excess moisture.

2. Meanwhile, place a griddle pan or frying pan over a high heat. Season the beef with salt and pepper, if using, lightly brush with oil and cook for 2–3 minutes on each side, turning once. Remove from the heat, cover with foil and leave to stand for 5 minutes.

3. Mix the parsley, mint, onion, tomatoes and bulgar wheat together in a bowl. Stir in the oil and lemon juice and season to taste with salt and pepper, if using.

4. Slice the beef into 2.5-cm/1-inch thick strips. Serve the bulgar wheat salad on a large serving platter and arrange the beef slices on top, then pour over the meat juices.

CHEESY BAKED COURGETTES

SERVES: *4* | **PREP:** *15 mins* | **COOK:** *15 mins*

INGREDIENTS

4 courgettes

2 tbsp extra virgin olive oil

115 g/4 oz mozzarella cheese,
*   thinly sliced*

2 large tomatoes, deseeded
*   and diced*

2 tsp chopped fresh basil or oregano

1. Preheat the oven to 200°C/400°F/Gas Mark 6. Slice each courgette lengthways into four strips, keeping the stem ends intact to hold them together. Spread the slices in a fan shape. Brush with oil and place on a large baking sheet.

2. Bake the courgettes in the preheated oven for 10 minutes until tender but not mushy.

3. Remove the courgettes from the oven. Arrange the cheese slices on top and sprinkle with the tomatoes and basil. Return to the oven and bake for 5 minutes, or until the cheese has melted and is beginning to turn golden.

4. Transfer to warmed serving plates and serve immediately.

FATTOUSH

SERVES: *4* | **PREP:** *15 mins* | **COOK:** *5 mins*

INGREDIENTS

1 small red pepper, halved,
deseeded and diced
1 small yellow pepper, halved,
deseeded and diced
1 small green pepper, halved,
deseeded and diced
300 g/10½ oz cucumber, peeled,
halved lengthways, deseeded and
diced
2 spring onions, finely chopped
25 g/1 oz fresh mint, finely chopped
25 g/1 oz fresh coriander, finely
chopped
2 pittas
85 g/3 oz feta cheese, crumbled
(drained weight)

DRESSING

juice of 1 lemon
3 tbsp olive oil
½ tsp cumin seeds, roughly crushed
1 garlic clove, finely chopped
pepper (optional)

1. Put the red, yellow and green peppers, the cucumber and spring onions into a salad bowl, sprinkle over the mint and coriander and gently toss together.

2. To make the dressing, put the lemon juice, oil, cumin and garlic in a jam jar, season with a little pepper, if using, screw on the lid and shake well. Drizzle the dressing over the salad and gently toss, then spoon into four bowls.

3. Preheat a griddle pan over a medium heat. Cook the pittas in the hot pan for 1½ minutes on each side until hot and puffy. Transfer to a plate and cut into small pieces. Sprinkle the pitta pieces and cheese over the salad and serve immediately.

TOMATO, OLIVE & MOZZARELLA PASTA SALAD

SERVES: 4 | **PREP:** 15 mins, plus cooling | **COOK:** 15 mins

INGREDIENTS

225 g/8 oz dried conchiglie
50 g/1¾ oz pine nuts
350 g/12 oz cherry tomatoes, halved
1 red pepper, deseeded and cut into
    bite-sized chunks
1 red onion, chopped
200 g/7 oz mozzarella cheese, cut
    into small pieces
12 black olives, stoned
25 g/1 oz fresh basil leaves
fresh Parmesan cheese shavings, to
    garnish
salt (optional)

DRESSING

5 tbsp extra virgin olive oil
2 tbsp balsamic vinegar
1 tbsp chopped fresh basil
salt and pepper (optional)

1. Add a little salt, if using, to a large saucepan of water and bring to the boil. Add the pasta, bring back to the boil and cook for 8–10 minutes until tender but still firm to the bite. Drain, refresh under cold running water and drain again. Leave to cool.

2. Meanwhile, heat a dry frying pan over a low heat, add the pine nuts and cook, shaking the pan frequently, for 1–2 minutes until lightly toasted. Remove the pan from the heat, transfer the pine nuts to a dish and leave to cool.

3. To make the dressing, put all the ingredients in a small bowl and mix together well. Cover with clingfilm and set aside.

4. Divide the pasta between four serving bowls. Add the pine nuts, tomatoes, pepper, onion, mozzarella and olives to each bowl. Sprinkle over the basil, then drizzle with the dressing. Garnish with cheese shavings and serve immediately.

ROASTED LEEKS
WITH PARSLEY

SERVES: *4* | **PREP:** *10 mins* | **COOK:** *15–20 mins*

INGREDIENTS

4 large leeks, trimmed and halved
*   lengthways*
3 tbsp extra virgin olive oil
1 tbsp chopped fresh flat-leaf
*   parsley*
sea salt flakes and pepper
(optional)

1. Preheat the oven to 240°C/475°/Gas Mark 9. Pack the leeks in a single layer in a shallow casserole into which they fit tightly.

2. Brush with the oil, taking care that it goes into the crevices. Sprinkle with the parsley, and salt and pepper, if using, turning to coat completely.

3. Roast in the preheated oven for 15–20 minutes, turning once, until the leeks begin to blacken at the edges. Serve.

STIR-FRIED BRUSSELS SPROUTS WITH ALMONDS

SERVES: *4* | **PREP:** *20 mins* | **COOK:** *15 mins*

INGREDIENTS

450 g/1 lb Brussels sprouts,
trimmed and quartered
2 tbsp groundnut oil
1 tbsp toasted sesame oil
1 shallot, finely chopped
3-cm/1¼-inch piece fresh ginger,
finely chopped
1 garlic clove, thinly sliced
3–4 tbsp chicken stock or vegetable
stock
juice of ½ lime
3 tbsp unskinned almonds, halved
lengthways
4 tbsp chopped fresh coriander
salt and pepper (optional)
lime wedges, to garnish

1. Bring a large saucepan of water to the boil. Add the Brussels sprouts and blanch for 3 minutes. Drain and rinse under cold running water, then pat dry with kitchen paper. Slice lengthways into quarters.

2. Heat a wok or large frying pan over a medium–high heat. Add the groundnut oil and sesame oil. Add the shallot, ginger and garlic and stir-fry for 1–2 minutes, or until the garlic is just starting to colour.

3. Add the sprouts, stock and lime juice. Season to taste with salt and pepper, if using, then stir-fry for 2–3 minutes until the sprouts are beginning to soften. Stir in the almonds and stir-fry for 1–2 minutes, or until the sprouts are tender but still bright green. Stir in the coriander, garnish with lime wedges and serve immediately.

ROOT VEGETABLE FRIES

SERVES: *4* | **PREP:** *10 mins* | **COOK:** *25 mins*

INGREDIENTS

225 g/8 oz parsnips, peeled and cut
into 5-mm/¼-inch strips
225 g/8 oz swedes, peeled and cut
into 5-mm/¼-inch strips
225 g/8 oz turnips, peeled and cut
into 5-mm/¼-inch strips
225 g/8 oz carrots, peeled and cut
into 5-mm/¼-inch strips
2 tbsp vegetable oil
1 tsp salt
sea salt (optional)

1. Preheat the oven to 230°C/450°F/Gas Mark 8.

2. Toss the vegetables with the oil and salt and spread in a single layer on a large baking sheet. Bake in the preheated oven for about 20 minutes, flipping them halfway through cooking, until golden brown and cooked through. Remove from the oven and preheat the grill to medium.

3. Place the vegetables under the preheated grill for 2–3 minutes until they begin to crisp up. Flip them over and return to the grill for a further 2 minutes to crisp the other side. Serve immediately, sprinkled with sea salt, if using.

FALAFEL PATTIES

SERVES: *4* | **PREP:** *15 mins* | **COOK:** *5 mins*

INGREDIENTS

800 g/1 lb 12 oz canned chickpeas,
*   drained and rinsed*
1 small onion, chopped
zest and juice of 1 lime
2 tsp ground coriander
2 tsp ground cumin
plain flour, for dusting
4 tbsp olive oil
fresh basil sprigs, to garnish
tomato salsa, to serve

1. Place the chickpeas, onion, lime zest and juice, coriander and cumin in a food processor or blender and process to a coarse paste. Transfer the mixture to a large mixing bowl.

2. Divide the mixture into eight balls, dust with flour, then flatten slightly to make a patty shape of your preferred thickness.

3. Heat the oil in a large frying pan over a medium heat. Add the patties and cook for 2 minutes. Turn and cook for a further 2 minutes until cooked through and crisp.

4. Transfer to warmed serving plates. Garnish with basil sprigs and serve with tomato salsa.

CHICKEN & HERB FRITTERS

SERVES: *4* | **PREP:** *20 mins* | **COOK:** *5–10 mins*

INGREDIENTS

500 g/1 lb 2 oz mashed potato

250 g/9 oz cooked chicken, chopped

125 g/4½ oz cooked ham, finely chopped

1 tbsp fresh mixed herbs

2 eggs, lightly beaten

1 tbsp milk

125 g/4½ oz fresh wholemeal breadcrumbs

oil, for shallow-frying

salt and pepper (optional)

mixed salad leaves, to serve

1. Place the potato, chicken, ham, herbs and one of the eggs in a large mixing bowl. Season to taste with salt and pepper, if using, and mix well together.

2. Divide the mixture into small portions and shape each into a ball.

3. Beat the remaining egg with the milk in a wide, shallow dish. Place the breadcrumbs in a separate wide, shallow dish.

4. Coat the chicken balls in the egg mixture, allowing any excess to drip back into the dish, then coat in the breadcrumbs.

5. Heat the oil in a large frying pan over a medium heat and cook the fritters until they are golden brown.

6. Transfer to a warmed serving dish and serve immediately with mixed salad leaves.

PORK SPRING ROLLS

MAKES: *20 spring rolls* | **PREP:** *20 mins* | **COOK:** *20 mins*

INGREDIENTS

6 dried Chinese mushrooms,
  soaked in warm water for 20
  minutes
1 tbsp vegetable oil or groundnut
  oil, plus extra for deep-frying
225 g/8 oz fresh pork mince
1 tsp dark soy sauce
100 g/3½ oz canned bamboo
  shoots, rinsed and julienned
pinch of salt
100 g/3½ oz raw prawns, peeled,
  deveined and chopped
225 g/8 oz beansprouts, trimmed
  and roughly chopped
1 tbsp finely chopped spring onions
20 spring roll wrappers
1 egg white, lightly beaten

1. Squeeze out any excess water from the mushrooms and finely slice, discarding any tough stems.

2. Heat a wok or large, heavy-based saucepan over a high heat, then add the oil. Add the pork and stir-fry until it is cooked through and no longer pink.

3. Add the soy sauce, bamboo shoots, mushrooms and salt and stir over a high heat for 3 minutes.

4. Add the prawns and cook for 2 minutes until they turn pink. Add the beansprouts and cook for a further 1 minute. Remove from the heat and stir in the spring onions.

5. Place a tablespoon of the mixture towards the bottom of a spring roll wrapper. Roll once to secure the filling, then fold in the sides to create a 10-cm/4-inch piece and continue to roll up. Seal the join with egg white.

6. Heat enough oil for deep-frying in a large wok or large, heavy-based saucepan to 180–190°C/350–375°F, or until a cube of bread browns in 30 seconds. Fry the rolls for about 5 minutes until golden brown and crispy. Serve hot.

POTATO FRITTERS WITH ONION & TOMATO RELISH

SERVES: 8 | **PREP:** 25 mins | **COOK:** 15–20 mins

INGREDIENTS

55 g/2 oz wholemeal flour
½ tsp ground coriander
½ tsp cumin seeds
¼ tsp chilli powder
½ tsp turmeric
¼ tsp salt
1 egg
3 tbsp milk
350 g/12 oz potatoes
1–2 garlic cloves, crushed
4 spring onions, chopped
55 g/2 oz sweetcorn kernels
vegetable oil, for shallow-frying

ONION & TOMATO RELISH

1 onion
225 g/8 oz tomatoes
2 tbsp chopped fresh coriander
2 tbsp chopped fresh mint
2 tbsp lemon juice
½ tsp roasted cumin seeds
¼ tsp salt
pinch of cayenne pepper

1. First, make the relish. Cut the onion and tomatoes into small dice and place in a bowl with the remaining ingredients. Mix well together and leave to stand for at least 15 minutes before serving to allow the flavours to blend.

2. Meanwhile, place the flour in a bowl, stir in the coriander, cumin seeds, chilli powder, turmeric and salt and make a well in the centre. Add the egg and milk and mix to a fairly thick batter.

3. Coarsely grate the potatoes, place them in a sieve and rinse well under cold running water. Drain and squeeze dry, then stir them into the batter with the garlic, spring onions and sweetcorn and mix to combine thoroughly.

4. Heat about 5 mm/¼ inch of oil in a large frying pan and add a few tablespoons of the mixture at a time, flattening each to form a thin cake. Fry over a low heat, turning frequently, for 2–3 minutes, or until golden brown and cooked through.

5. Drain the fritters on kitchen paper and keep warm while frying the remaining mixture. Serve hot with the relish.

BAKED FIGS WITH GORGONZOLA

SERVES: *4* | **PREP:** *15 mins* | **COOK:** *10 mins*

INGREDIENTS

*1 mixed-grain demi baguette, cut
into 8 x 2-cm/¾-inch thick slices
(total weight 100 g/3½ oz)*
8 small fresh figs
*55 g/2 oz Gorgonzola cheese, rind
removed, cut into 8 squares*
4 tsp clear wild-flower honey

1. Preheat the oven to 180°C/350°F/Gas Mark 4. Lightly toast the
bread on both sides, then transfer to a small baking sheet.

2. Cut a cross in the top of each fig, lightly press a cube of cheese into
each one, then place a fig on top of each slice of toast. Bake in the
preheated oven for 5–6 minutes until the figs are hot and the cheese
is just melting.

3. Transfer to a plate or chopping board. Drizzle with honey and
serve immediately.

LAMB KOFTAS WITH YOGURT, THYME & LEMON DIP

SERVES: *4* | **PREP:** *20 mins* | **COOK:** *12–15 mins*

INGREDIENTS

500 g/1 lb 2 oz fresh lean lamb
  mince
25 g/1 oz fresh white breadcrumbs
1 onion, grated
1 garlic clove, crushed
1 tsp ground coriander
1 tsp ground cumin
2 tbsp chopped fresh mint
olive oil, for brushing
salt and pepper (optional)
lemon wedges, to serve

YOGURT, THYME & LEMON DIP

150 ml/5 fl oz natural yogurt
finely grated rind and juice of ½
  lemon
1 tbsp chopped fresh thyme
salt and pepper (optional)

1. Put the mince, breadcrumbs, onion, garlic, coriander, cumin and mint into a bowl and mix together. Season well with salt and pepper, if using.

2. Divide the mixture into eight equal portions and press evenly onto eight pre-soaked wooden skewers or metal skewers.

3. To make the yogurt, thyme and lemon dip, put the yogurt and lemon rind and juice into a bowl and mix together. Stir in the thyme and season to taste with salt and pepper, if using.

4. Heat a ridged griddle pan over a medium–high heat. Brush the koftas with oil, place in the pan and cook, turning occasionally, for 10–12 minutes until golden brown and cooked through. Serve with the thyme and lemon dip and lemon wedges.

CANNELLINI BEAN DIP
WITH CRUDITÉS

SERVES: *4* | **PREP:** *15 mins* | **COOK:** *5 mins*

INGREDIENTS

1 wholemeal pitta
⅓ cucumber, quartered lengthways,
deseeded and cut into sticks
3 celery sticks, halved lengthways
and cut into batons
4 radishes, quartered

DIP

400 g/14 oz canned cannellini
beans in water, drained and
rinsed
3 garlic cloves, crushed
juice of ½ lemon
2½ tbsp olive oil
1 tsp salt
pepper (optional)

1. To make the dip, put the beans into the bowl of a food processor. Add the garlic, lemon juice, oil, salt, and pepper, if using. Pulse for 20 seconds, or until a thick paste forms. Alternatively, place the ingredients in a mixing bowl and beat thoroughly with a wooden spoon to combine. Add a little water if the mixture is too stiff. Transfer to a small bowl.

2. Preheat the grill to medium and lightly toast the pitta. Cut into eight strips.

3. Place the bowl of dip in the centre of a plate, surrounded by the crudités and pitta strips. Serve immediately.

BAKED CHICKEN WINGS

SERVES: *4* | **PREP:** *15 mins* | **COOK:** *20 mins*

INGREDIENTS

12 chicken wings

1 egg

4 tbsp milk

70 g/2½ oz plain flour

1 tsp paprika

225 g/8 oz breadcrumbs

55 g/2 oz butter

salt and pepper (optional)

1. Preheat the oven to 220°C/425°F/Gas Mark 7. Separate each chicken wing into three pieces, discarding the bony tip. Beat the egg with the milk in a shallow dish.

2. Combine the flour, paprika, and salt and pepper to taste, if using, in a shallow dish. Place the breadcrumbs in a separate dish. Dip the chicken in the egg mixture, drain and roll in the flour.

3. Shake off any excess, then roll the chicken wings in the breadcrumbs, gently pressing them onto the surface and shaking off any excess.

4. Put the butter in a wide, shallow roasting tin and place in the preheated oven to melt. Place the chicken in the tin skin side down.

5. Bake for 10 minutes on each side. To check the wings are cooked through, cut into the middle and ensure there are no remaining traces of pink or red. Any juices that run out should be clear and piping hot with visible steam rising.

6. To serve, transfer the chicken to a warmed serving platter.

CHICKEN NUGGETS
WITH BARBECUE SAUCE

SERVES: *4* | **PREP:** *15 mins* | **COOK:** *15 mins*

INGREDIENTS

4 tbsp dry breadcrumbs

*2 tbsp freshly grated Parmesan
  cheese*

2 tsp chopped fresh thyme

2 boneless chicken breasts

115 g/4 oz melted butter

salt and pepper (optional)

BARBECUE SAUCE

55 g/2 oz butter

2 large onions, grated

300 ml/10 fl oz cider vinegar

300 ml/10 fl oz tomato ketchup

175 g/6 oz dark brown sugar

1–2 tsp Worcestershire sauce

salt and pepper (optional)

1. Preheat the oven to 200°C/400°F/Gas Mark 6. Place the breadcrumbs, cheese and thyme in a wide, shallow bowl. Season to taste with salt and pepper, if using, and mix together.

2. Remove any skin from the chicken and cut into cubes. Coat the pieces in the melted butter, allowing any excess to drip back into the dish, then coat in the crumb mixture.

3. Arrange the chicken pieces in a single layer on a large baking sheet. Bake in the preheated oven for 10 minutes until the chicken is cooked through.

4. Meanwhile, to make the sauce, heat the butter in a large saucepan over a low heat. Add the onions and cook until soft but not brown. Add the cider vinegar, tomato ketchup, sugar and Worcestershire sauce. Season to taste with salt and pepper, if using, and heat, stirring, until the sugar has completely dissolved. Bring to the boil, then reduce the heat and simmer for 5 minutes.

5. Transfer the chicken to a warmed serving dish and serve immediately with the sauce.

FETA & OLIVE SCONES

SERVES: *8* | **PREP:** *20 mins* | **COOK:** *12–15 mins*

INGREDIENTS

400 g/14 oz self-raising flour, plus extra for dusting

¼ tsp salt

85 g/3 oz butter, plus extra for greasing and serving

40 g/1½ oz stoned black olives, chopped

40 g/1½ oz sun-dried tomatoes in oil, drained and chopped

85 g/3 oz feta cheese, crumbled

200 ml/7 fl oz milk, plus extra for glazing

pepper (optional)

1. Preheat the oven to 220°C/425°F/Gas Mark 7 and lightly grease a baking sheet.

2. Sift the flour, salt, and pepper to taste, if using, into a bowl and evenly rub in the butter with your fingertips.

3. Stir in the olives, tomatoes and cheese, then stir in just enough milk to make a soft, smooth dough.

4. Turn out the dough onto a floured work surface and roll out to a 3-cm/1¼-inch thick rectangle. Cut into eight 6-cm/2½-inch squares. Place on the baking sheet, brush with milk and bake in the preheated oven for 12–15 minutes until golden.

5. Serve warm with butter.

APPLE & PEANUT BUTTER SANDWICHES

SERVES: *4* | **PREP:** *20 mins* | **COOK:** *No cooking*

INGREDIENTS

2 green-skinned dessert apples

2 red-skinned dessert apples

juice of 2 lemons

115 g/4 oz crunchy peanut butter

4 tbsp dried cranberries, roughly chopped

2 tbsp sunflower seeds

2 tbsp porridge oats

60 g/2¼ oz dried apricots, diced

35 g/1¼ oz unblanched hazelnuts, roughly chopped

1. Cut each apple into six slices, then remove any pips (there is no need to core them). Put the apple pieces into a bowl, add the lemon juice and turn to coat evenly, to prevent discoloration.

2. Drain the apples, place on a tray or chopping board and spread each slice with peanut butter. Sprinkle half the slices with the cranberries, sunflower seeds, oats, apricots and hazelnuts.

3. Cover with the remaining apple slices, peanut butter side down, and press together to make sandwiches. Serve immediately.

SPICE-ROASTED EDAMAME & CRANBERRIES

SERVES: *4* | **PREP:** *15 mins* | **COOK:** *15 mins*

INGREDIENTS

350 g/12 oz frozen edamame (soya) beans

5-cm/2-inch piece fresh ginger, peeled and finely grated

1 tsp Sichuan peppercorns, roughly crushed

1 tbsp soy sauce

1 tbsp olive oil

3 small star anise

40 g/1½ oz dried cranberries

1. Preheat the oven to 180°C/350°F/Gas Mark 4. Place the beans in a roasting tin, then sprinkle over the ginger and peppercorns, drizzle with soy sauce and oil and mix together.

2. Tuck the star anise in among the beans, then roast, uncovered, in the preheated oven for 15 minutes.

3. Stir in the cranberries and leave to cool. Spoon into a small jar and eat within 12 hours.

CHAPTER THREE

LUNCH

TURKEY MISO SOUP

INGREDIENTS

225 g/8 oz fresh udon noodles

1 tbsp vegetable oil

1 small leek, halved lengthways and
thinly sliced

2.4 litres/4 pints turkey stock

3 carrots, sliced

1 tsp white pepper

225 g/8 oz sugar snap peas, halved

280 g/10 oz cooked turkey meat,
shredded or chopped

4 tbsp white miso paste

1. Cook the noodles according to the packet instructions.

2. Heat the oil in a medium-sized saucepan over a medium–high heat. Add the leek and cook, stirring frequently, for 3 minutes, or until it begins to soften. Add the stock, carrots and pepper and bring to the boil. Reduce the heat to low and simmer for 15 minutes, or until the carrots are just tender.

3. Add the sugar snap peas, turkey and cooked noodles and simmer for 2–3 minutes until heated through. Stir in the miso paste until it has dissolved.

4. Transfer the soup to warmed bowls and serve immediately.

LEMON, CHICKEN & RICE SOUP

INGREDIENTS

1 tbsp vegetable oil
1 onion, finely chopped
1 leek, finely chopped
1 garlic clove, crushed
finely grated zest and juice of
　½ lemon
100 g/3½ oz basmati rice
1 litre/1¾ pints chicken stock
2 cooked chicken breasts, roughly
　chopped
100 g/3½ oz fresh spinach
175 g/6 oz frozen peas
4 tbsp chopped fresh flat-leaf
　parsley
salt and pepper (optional)
Parmesan cheese shavings, to serve

1. Heat the oil in a large saucepan over a medium heat. Add the onion and leek and sauté for 4–5 minutes until beginning to soften. Add the garlic and lemon zest and cook for a further 1–2 minutes.

2. Add the rice and stock and bring to the boil. Cover and simmer for 8 minutes. Add the chicken, spinach and peas and season to taste with salt and pepper, if using. Cook for a further 4 minutes until the rice is cooked through.

3. Stir in the lemon juice and parsley and serve with some Parmesan cheese shavings scattered on top.

QUICK TOMATO SOUP

SERVES: *4* | **PREP:** *10 mins* | **COOK:** *30 mins*

INGREDIENTS

2 tbsp olive oil

1 large onion, chopped

*400 g/14 oz canned whole plum
    tomatoes*

300 ml/10 fl oz vegetable stock

1 tbsp tomato purée

1 tsp hot pepper sauce

handful of fresh basil leaves

salt and pepper (optional)

1. Heat the oil in a large saucepan over a medium heat, then add the onion and fry, stirring, for 4–5 minutes until soft. Add the tomatoes, stock, tomato purée, hot pepper sauce and half the basil leaves.

2. Process using a hand-held blender until smooth. Stir the soup over a medium heat until just boiling, then season to taste with salt and pepper, if using.

3. Serve in warmed bowls, garnished with the remaining basil leaves.

SPICY CHICKEN NOODLE SOUP

SERVES: *2* | **PREP:** *15 mins* | **COOK:** *10–15 mins*

INGREDIENTS

300 ml/10 fl oz chicken stock

250 ml/9 fl oz boiling water

18 g/¾ oz miso paste

2-cm/¾-inch piece fresh ginger, peeled and finely grated

1 red chilli, deseeded and thinly sliced

1 carrot, cut into thin strips

200 g/7 oz pak choi, roughly chopped

150 g/5½ oz dried egg thread noodles, cooked

1 cooked chicken breast, shredded

dark soy sauce, to taste

4 spring onions, trimmed and finely chopped

handful of fresh coriander, roughly chopped, to serve

1. Place the stock and boiling water in a saucepan and bring to the boil over a medium–high heat. Add the miso paste and simmer for 1–2 minutes.

2. Add the ginger, chilli, carrot, pak choi, noodles and chicken to the pan and simmer for a further 4–5 minutes, then season to taste with soy sauce.

3. Scatter the spring onions in the base of two warmed bowls and pour the soup over. Top the soup with the chopped coriander and serve immediately.

GREEN GODDESS SALAD

SERVES: *4* | **PREP:** *10–15 mins* | **COOK:** *10–15 mins*

INGREDIENTS

200 g/7 oz frozen edamame beans,
* or shelled broad beans*
115 g/4 oz French beans
500 g/1 lb 2 oz fresh peas, shelled
50 g/1¾ oz pea shoots
50 g/1¾ oz ready-to-eat sprouting
* seeds, such as alfalfa and radish*

DRESSING

2 tbsp rice bran oil
2 tbsp olive oil
juice of 1 lime
1 tsp agave syrup
2-cm/¾-inch piece fresh ginger,
* peeled and finely grated*
salt and pepper (optional)

1. Bring a saucepan of water to the boil, add the edamame beans and French beans and simmer for 2 minutes. Add any pea pods and simmer for a further 1 minute. Drain through a sieve, cool under cold running water and drain again. Transfer to a salad bowl and sprinkle over the raw peas.

2. To make the dressing, put the rice bran oil, olive oil, lime juice, agave syrup and ginger in a jam jar, season with a little salt and pepper, if using, screw on the lid and shake well.

3. Drizzle the dressing over the salad and gently toss together. Top with the pea shoots and sprouting seeds and serve immediately.

GREEK SALAD

SERVES: *4* | **PREP:** *15 mins* | **COOK:** *No cooking*

INGREDIENTS

6–8 vine leaves
4 tomatoes, sliced
½ cucumber, peeled and sliced
1 small red onion, thinly sliced
115 g/4 oz feta cheese, cubed
8 black olives

DRESSING

3 tbsp extra virgin olive oil
1 tbsp lemon juice
½ tsp dried oregano
salt and pepper (optional)

1. To make the dressing, blend the oil, lemon juice and oregano with salt and pepper, if using, in a small bowl, or put into a screw-top jar and shake until well blended.

2. Arrange the vine leaves on a serving dish, then add the tomatoes, cucumber and onion. Scatter the cheese and olives on top.

3. Pour the dressing over the salad and serve immediately.

TURKEY & CRANBERRY SALAD

INGREDIENTS

150 g/5½ oz brown basmati rice
40 g/1½ oz wild rice
250 g/9 oz turkey breast, sliced
40 g/1½ oz dried cranberries
3 spring onions, finely chopped
200 g/7 oz tomatoes, diced
1 small red pepper, halved,
*   deseeded and cut into chunks*
55 g/2 oz rocket
40 g/1½ oz wafer-thin sliced lean
*   ready-to-eat ham, cut into strips*
salt and pepper (optional)

DRESSING

1½ tbsp cranberry sauce
1½ tbsp sherry vinegar
finely grated rind and juice of
*   1 small unwaxed lemon*
1 tbsp Dijon mustard
salt and pepper (optional)

1. Put cold water in the base of a steamer, bring to the boil, then add the brown rice and wild rice and bring back to the boil. Put the turkey in the top of the steamer in a single layer, season with salt and pepper, if using. Put it in the steamer base, cover and steam for 15 minutes, or until the turkey is cooked; cut into the middle of a slice to check that the meat is no longer pink and that the juices are clear and piping hot. Remove the steamer top and cook the rice for a further 5–10 minutes, or until tender.

2. Dice the turkey and put it in a bowl. Add the cranberries. Drain and rinse the rice, then add to the bowl.

3. To make the dressing, put the cranberry sauce in a small saucepan and place over a low heat until just melted. Remove from the heat, then add the vinegar, lemon rind and juice, mustard, and a little salt and pepper, if using. Whisk together until smooth, then drizzle over the salad and leave to cool.

4. Add the spring onions, tomatoes and red pepper to the salad. Gently toss together, then divide between four plates. Top with the rocket and ham and serve.

PAPRIKA STEAK WRAPS WITH HORSERADISH CREAM

SERVES: *4* | **PREP:** *15 mins* | **COOK:** *10 mins, plus resting*

INGREDIENTS

4 sirloin steaks, about 175 g/6 oz
*   each*
1 garlic clove, crushed
2 tsp smoked paprika, plus extra
*   for sprinkling*
sunflower oil, for brushing
100 g/3½ oz crème fraîche
3 tbsp creamed horseradish
8 small flour tortillas
75 g/2¾ oz rocket
2 ripe avocados, stoned, peeled
*   and sliced*
1 red onion, thinly sliced
salt and pepper (optional)

1. Spread the steaks with the garlic and sprinkle both sides with the paprika. Season to taste with salt and pepper, if using.

2. Preheat a ridged griddle pan over a very high heat and brush with oil. Add the steaks and cook for 6–8 minutes, turning once. Remove from the heat and leave to rest for 5 minutes.

3. Meanwhile, place the crème fraîche and horseradish in a small bowl and mix together. Using half the horseradish cream, spread a thin layer over each tortilla.

4. Slice the steaks into strips. Divide between the tortillas and add the rocket, avocado and red onion, wrapping the sides over. Serve immediately with an extra spoonful of horseradish cream, sprinkled with a little more paprika.

ITALIAN SAUSAGE SUBS

SERVES: *4* | **PREP:** *10–15 mins* | **COOK:** *30 mins*

INGREDIENTS

2 tbsp olive oil

8 Italian sausages

1 green pepper

1 red pepper

1 orange pepper

1 onion

2 garlic cloves

½ tsp salt

½ tsp pepper

125 ml/4 fl oz red wine

400 g/14 oz canned chopped
  tomatoes

2 tsp dried oregano

4 submarine rolls

TO SERVE

280 g/10 oz rocket

salad dressing

mayonnaise

1. Heat the oil in a large frying pan over a medium–high heat. Add the sausages and cook, turning occasionally, for 6–8 minutes until brown all over. Remove from the pan and set aside. Meanwhile, deseed the green, red and orange peppers and slice them into 2.5-cm/1-inch wide strips. Halve the onion and thinly slice into half circles. Finely chop the garlic.

2. Add the peppers and onion to the pan and cook, stirring frequently, for about 4 minutes, until they begin to soften, then add the garlic, salt and pepper. Cook, stirring, for a further 1–2 minutes. Add the wine, tomatoes and oregano and bring to the boil. Return the sausages to the pan, cover and cook for about 15 minutes until the sausages are cooked through.

3. Split the rolls and spoon some vegetables into each. Place two sausages on top and serve hot with rocket, salad dressing and mayonnaise on the side.

MEATBALL SANDWICH

INGREDIENTS

400 g/14 oz fresh lean beef mince

1 onion, grated

1 garlic clove, crushed

2 tsp mild chilli powder

25 g/1 oz fresh wholemeal
*   breadcrumbs*

oil, for shallow-frying

salt and pepper (optional)

TO SERVE

lettuce leaves

4 sub rolls, halved lengthways

1 red onion, thinly sliced into rings

1. Place the mince in a large mixing bowl. Add the onion, garlic, chilli powder and breadcrumbs. Season to taste with salt and pepper, if using, and mix together. Use a small ice-cream scoop to shape the mixture into small balls.

2. Heat a shallow depth of oil in a deep frying pan until very hot. Add the meatballs in batches and fry for 8–10 minutes, or until they are cooked through.

3. Lift out the meatballs with a slotted spoon and drain on absorbent kitchen paper.

4. Place the lettuce leaves on the bottom halves of the rolls and top with the meatballs. Place the onion rings on top, cover with the lids and serve immediately.

FALAFEL PITTA POCKETS

SERVES: *4* | **PREP:** *20 mins* | **COOK:** *10 mins*

INGREDIENTS

2 garlic cloves

*2 tbsp chopped fresh flat-leaf
    parsley*

1 tsp ground cumin

½ tsp salt

*275 g/9¾ oz canned chickpeas,
    drained and rinsed*

2 spring onions, sliced

2 tbsp plain flour

1 tsp baking powder

1 tbsp vegetable oil

TO SERVE

2 wholemeal pittas

tzatziki dip

diced tomatoes

shredded lettuce

1. To make the falafel patties, chop the garlic in a food processor. Add the parsley, cumin and salt and process until finely chopped. Add the chickpeas, spring onions, flour and baking powder and process until the texture resembles coarse breadcrumbs. Shape the falafel mixture into eight patties, about 5 mm/¼ inch thick.

2. In a heavy-based frying pan, heat the oil over a medium–high heat. Add the patties and cook for about 3 minutes, or until brown on the base. Turn and cook until brown on the other side. Remove from the pan with a slotted spatula and drain on kitchen paper.

3. To serve, stuff two falafel patties into each pitta half, drizzle with some tzatziki dip, then add diced tomato and shredded lettuce. Serve immediately.

MINI PIZZA MUFFINS

SERVES: *2* | **PREP:** *10 mins* | **COOK:** *15 mins*

INGREDIENTS

2 wholemeal English muffins

*125 g/4½ oz ready-made tomato
    pasta sauce with mushrooms*

1 tomato, sliced

*80 g/2¾ oz chestnut mushrooms,
    sliced*

*1 ready-roasted green or yellow
    pepper in water, drained and
    sliced, 100 g/3½ oz drained
    weight*

2 slices Parma ham, torn in half

*125 g/4½ oz mozzarella cheese,
    sliced*

8 black olives, stoned and sliced

1. Preheat the oven to 180°C/350°F/Gas Mark 4. Split the muffins and arrange the halves cut side up on a baking tray.

2. Spread a thin layer of tomato sauce on the muffin halves, then top with the sliced tomato and mushrooms.

3. Divide the green pepper between the muffin halves, then top with the ham, cheese and black olives.

4. Bake in the preheated oven for 15 minutes, or until the cheese is melted and the muffins are toasted. Serve immediately.

CHIPOTLE PORK FAJITAS

SERVES: *4* | **PREP:** *20 mins* | **COOK:** *20–25 mins*

INGREDIENTS

8–12 flour tortillas
1 tbsp ground chipotle chilli
2 tsp soft light brown sugar
1 tsp salt
1 tsp ground cumin
1 tsp dried oregano
½ tsp garlic powder
1 pork fillet
2 bacon rashers
1 onion
1 red pepper
1 orange or yellow pepper
1 tbsp olive oil
1 tbsp garlic purée
fresh mint leaves, to garnish

TO SERVE

salsa
chopped avocado
soured cream
lime halves

1. Preheat the oven to 200°C/400°F/Gas Mark 6, wrap the tortillas in foil and place in the oven to warm. Combine the chilli, sugar, salt, cumin, oregano and garlic powder in a small bowl.

2. Slice the pork into 5-mm/¼-inch thick rounds, then cut the rounds into 1-cm/½-inch wide strips. Dice the bacon. Put the pork and bacon into a large bowl with the spice mixture and toss. Slice the onion, red pepper and orange pepper into 1-cm/½-inch wide strips.

3. Heat the oil in a large frying pan over a medium–high heat. Add the pork and bacon and cook, stirring, for 4–5 minutes until the meat is brown. Transfer to a plate. Add the onion, garlic purée and peppers to the pan and cook for about 4 minutes until the vegetables begin to soften. Return the meat to the pan and fry until cooked through.

4. Garnish with fresh mint leaves and serve immediately with the warmed tortillas, salsa, avocado, soured cream and lime halves.

MOROCCAN MEATBALLS WITH MINT YOGURT

SERVES: *4* | **PREP:** *20–25 mins* | **COOK:** *15 mins*

INGREDIENTS

olive oil spray, for oiling
½ small onion
1 garlic clove
450 g/1 lb fresh lamb mince
1½ tsp ground cumin
1 tsp salt
½ tsp pepper
¼ tsp ground cinnamon
1 egg
10 g/¼ oz fresh breadcrumbs
4 pittas, to serve

MINT YOGURT

10 g/¼ oz fresh mint leaves
280 g/10 oz natural yogurt
juice of ½ lemon
½ tsp salt
⅛ tsp cayenne pepper

SALAD

1 cucumber
140 g/5 oz cherry tomatoes
juice of 1 lemon
2 tbsp chopped fresh flat-leaf
*   parsley*
½ tsp salt

1. Preheat the oven to 190°C/375°F/Gas Mark 5. Line a large baking sheet with baking paper and spray with oil. Finely chop the onion and garlic. Put the lamb, onion, garlic, cumin, salt, pepper, cinnamon, egg and breadcrumbs into a large bowl, mix well to combine and shape into 2.5-cm/1-inch balls. Place the meatballs on the prepared baking sheet and spray with oil. Bake in the preheated oven for about 15 minutes until cooked through.

2. Meanwhile, wrap the pittas in foil and put them in the oven. To make the mint yogurt, finely chop the mint and put into a small bowl with the remaining ingredients. Stir to combine.

3. To make the salad, dice the cucumber and halve the tomatoes. Put them into a medium-sized bowl and mix to combine. Add the lemon juice, parsley and salt and stir to combine.

4. Remove the meatballs and bread from the oven. Cut the pittas in half. Stuff a few meatballs into each half and spoon in some of the mint yogurt. Serve two halves per person with the salad on the side.

FISH TACOS WITH AVOCADO SALSA

SERVES: *4* | **PREP:** *20 mins* | **COOK:** *10–15 mins*

INGREDIENTS

2 tbsp lime juice

1 tbsp olive oil

1 tsp ground cumin

1 tsp chilli powder

½ tsp salt

400 g/14 oz white fish fillets

SALSA

½ red onion, diced

2 jalapeño peppers, deseeded and diced

2 tomatoes, diced

½ avocado, diced

2 tbsp chopped fresh coriander

3 tbsp lime juice

½ tsp salt

TO SERVE

8 small corn tortillas (25 g/1 oz each)

300 g/10½ oz red cabbage, shredded

1. To make the salsa, put all the ingredients in a mixing bowl and stir well to combine.

2. Preheat the grill to medium–high or place a ridged griddle pan over a medium–high heat. In a small bowl, combine the lime juice, oil, cumin, chilli powder and salt.

3. Brush the lime mixture on both sides of the fish fillets. Grill the fish for 2–4 minutes on each side, or until grill marks appear and the fish is opaque and cooked through. Chop into bite-sized chunks.

4. To serve, warm the tortillas under the grill, then top them with the fish, salsa and shredded cabbage. Serve immediately with extra salsa on the side.

GRILLED HALLOUMI KEBABS
WITH FENNEL & WHITE BEANS

SERVES: *4* | **PREP:** *20 mins* | **COOK:** *10–15 mins*

INGREDIENTS

200 g/7 oz halloumi cheese
1 garlic clove, crushed
1 fennel bulb, thinly sliced
1 small red onion, thinly sliced
400 g/14 oz canned cannellini
*   beans, drained*
1–2 tbsp balsamic vinegar, to serve

DRESSING

finely grated rind and juice of
*   1 lemon*
3 tbsp chopped fresh flat-leaf
*   parsley*
4 tbsp olive oil
salt and pepper (optional)

1. To make the dressing, mix the lemon rind and juice, parsley and oil together with salt and pepper to taste, if using.

2. Cut the cheese into 2-cm/¾-inch cubes, thread onto four pre-soaked wooden skewers and brush with half the dressing.

3. Preheat a ridged griddle pan over a high heat. Cook the skewers in the pan, turning once, for 6–8 minutes until golden.

4. Heat the remaining dressing and the garlic in a small saucepan until boiling. Combine with the fennel, onion and beans.

5. Serve the skewers with the salad, sprinkled with balsamic vinegar.

SPICY TUNA FISHCAKES

SERVES: *4* | **PREP:** *15 mins* | **COOK:** *7–10 mins*

INGREDIENTS

*200 g/7 oz canned tuna in oil,
  drained*
200 g/7 oz mashed potato
2–3 tbsp curry paste
*1 spring onion, trimmed and finely
  chopped*
1 egg, beaten
*4 tbsp plain flour, plus extra for
  dusting*
*sunflower oil or groundnut oil, for
  frying*
salt and pepper (optional)
*rocket leaves and lemon wedges,
  to serve*

1. Place the tuna in a large mixing bowl. Add the potato, curry paste, spring onion and egg. Season to taste with salt and pepper, if using, and mix together.

2. Divide the mixture into four portions and shape each into a ball. On a floured surface, flatten them slightly to make patty shapes of your preferred thickness. Season the flour to taste with salt and pepper, if using. Turn each patty in the flour to coat.

3. Heat the oil in a large frying pan, add the patties and fry for 3–4 minutes on each side until crisp and golden.

4. Transfer to warmed serving plates and serve immediately with rocket leaves and lemon wedges.

PRAWNS WITH SMOKED PAPRIKA

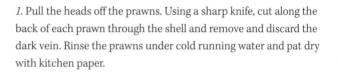

SERVES: *2* | **PREP:** *15 mins, plus marinating* | **COOK:** *5–6 mins*

INGREDIENTS

450 g/1 lb large raw unpeeled
*   prawns (about 12 prawns)*
2 tbsp olive oil
1 tbsp lemon juice
1½ tsp smoked paprika
1 garlic clove, peeled and crushed
sea salt (optional)
lemon wedges and crusty bread,
*   to serve*

1. Pull the heads off the prawns. Using a sharp knife, cut along the back of each prawn through the shell and remove and discard the dark vein. Rinse the prawns under cold running water and pat dry with kitchen paper.

2. Mix the oil, lemon juice, paprika and garlic together in a large bowl. Add a generous pinch of salt, if using, and the prepared prawns. Toss together. Set aside in a cool place to marinate for 15–20 minutes, stirring occasionally.

3. To cook, heat a ridged griddle pan over a high heat until smoking, then spread the prawns in a single layer in the pan and cook, turning once, for 3–4 minutes until they turn pink and are just cooked through. Serve immediately with lemon wedges and crusty bread.

PARMA HAM &
RED PEPPER PIZZA

MAKES: *1 pizza* | **PREP:** *15 mins* | **COOK:** *10 mins*

INGREDIENTS

2 tbsp olive oil

*30-cm/12-inch ready-made pizza
  base*

4 tbsp ready-made red pesto sauce

*1 small red pepper, deseeded and
  thinly sliced*

4 thin slices Parma ham

*100 g/3½ oz cherry plum tomatoes,
  halved*

*100 g/3½ oz mozzarella cheese,
  torn into pieces*

1 tsp dried oregano

salt and pepper (optional)

1. Preheat the oven to 220°C/425°F/Gas Mark 7. Brush a large baking sheet with a little oil and place the pizza base on the sheet.

2. Spread the pesto sauce over the pizza base to within 1-cm/½-inch of the edge. Arrange the red pepper slices, ham and tomatoes on top.

3. Scatter with the cheese, oregano, and salt and pepper to taste, if using, then drizzle over the remaining oil.

4. Bake in the preheated oven for about 10 minutes until bubbling and golden. Serve immediately.

CHILLI LAMB CUTLETS

SERVES: *4* | **PREP:** *15 mins* | **COOK:** *15–20 mins, plus resting*

INGREDIENTS

60 g/2¼ oz fresh flat-leaf parsley

2 garlic cloves

juice of 1 lemon

1–2 red or green chillies

1 tbsp sweet paprika

4 tbsp olive oil

4 x 5-cm/2-inch thick lamb cutlets

salt and pepper (optional)

pittas, to serve

SALAD

1 cucumber

1 tbsp fresh flat-leaf parsley

225 g/8 oz cherry tomatoes

juice of 1 lemon

½ tsp salt

1. Put the parsley, garlic, lemon juice, chillies, paprika and 1 teaspoon of salt, if using, into a food processor and process until smooth. Add the oil and process to combine. Season the lamb with salt and pepper, if using, then coat on both sides with some of the sauce. Reserve the remaining sauce.

2. To make the salad, dice the cucumber, finely chop the parsley and halve the tomatoes, then put them all into a medium-sized bowl. Toss with the lemon juice and salt, and set aside until ready to serve.

3. Heat a ridged griddle pan over a medium–high heat. Add the cutlets and cook for about 6 minutes on each side for medium-rare, or a bit longer for medium. Remove from the heat and leave to rest for a few minutes before serving. Meanwhile, warm the pittas under the grill. Serve the chops with the pittas, salad and reserved sauce.

CHAPTER FOUR

DINNER

• • •

MIXED BEAN, NUT
& KALE STEW

SERVES: *4* | **PREP:** *10 mins* | **COOK:** *30 mins*

INGREDIENTS

1 tbsp olive oil, for sautéing
1 large onion, peeled and chopped
2 garlic cloves, peeled and sliced
1 tsp smoked paprika
200 g/7 oz broad beans
400 g/14 oz canned butter beans,
*   drained and rinsed*
100 g/3½ oz French beans, trimmed
*   and halved*
400 g/14 oz canned chopped
*   tomatoes*
200 ml/7 fl oz vegetable stock
150 g/5½ oz kale, shredded
2 tbsp walnuts, chopped
1 tbsp Brazil nuts, chopped
1 tbsp hazelnuts, chopped
175 g/6 oz feta cheese, crumbled
salt and pepper (optional)
1 tbsp chopped fresh mint, to
*   garnish*
1 tbsp extra virgin olive oil, to serve

1. Heat the olive oil in a large pan, add the onion and sauté over a medium heat for 2–3 minutes. Stir in the garlic and paprika and cook for a further 1 minute.

2. Stir the beans, tomatoes and stock into the pan and bring to a simmer. Cook for 15 minutes, then stir in the kale and cook for a further 10 minutes. Season to taste with salt and pepper, if using.

3. Toast the nuts in a dry pan over a medium heat for 2–3 minutes.

4. Ladle the stew into four bowls and serve topped with the toasted nuts, cheese, chopped mint and a drizzle of extra virgin olive oil.

RICE & LENTIL CURRY

INGREDIENTS

2.5-cm/1-inch piece fresh ginger

2 garlic cloves

1 onion, diced

2 tbsp curry powder

1 tsp salt

2 carrots, diced

225 g/8 oz cauliflower

225 g/8 oz kale

2 tbsp olive oil

90 g/3¼ oz basmati rice

90 g/3¼ oz small green lentils or red lentils

700 ml/1¼ pints vegetable stock or water

125 ml/4 fl oz coconut milk

juice of 1 lime

natural yogurt and sriracha sauce, to serve

1. Peel and finely chop the ginger and garlic. Dice the onion and carrots. Chop the cauliflower into small pieces. Trim the thick stems and centre ribs from the kale leaves and cut the leaves into ribbons.

2. Heat the oil in a large frying pan over a medium–high heat. Add the ginger, garlic and onion and cook, stirring, for about 2 minutes until the onion begins to soften. Stir in the curry powder and salt. Add the vegetables, rice, lentils, stock and coconut milk and bring to the boil.

3. Reduce the heat to low, cover and simmer for 15–20 minutes until the lentils and rice are tender. Juice the lime and stir in. Serve immediately topped with yogurt and sriracha sauce.

PAPPARDELLE WITH CHERRY TOMATOES, ROCKET & MOZZARELLA

SERVES: *4* | **PREP:** *15 mins* | **COOK:** *13–15 mins*

INGREDIENTS

400 g/14 oz dried pappardelle
2 tbsp olive oil
1 garlic clove, chopped
350 g/12 oz cherry tomatoes, halved
85 g/3 oz rocket leaves
300 g/10½ oz mozzarella cheese,
*   chopped*
salt and pepper (optional)
freshly grated Parmesan cheese, to
*   serve*

1. Add a little salt, if using, to a large saucepan of water and bring to the boil. Add the pasta, bring back to the boil and cook for 8–10 minutes until tender but still firm to the bite.

2. Meanwhile, heat the oil in a frying pan over a medium heat, add the garlic and fry, stirring, for 1 minute, without browning.

3. Add the tomatoes, season to taste with salt and pepper, if using, and gently cook for 2–3 minutes until soft.

4. Drain the pasta and stir into the frying pan. Add the rocket leaves and mozzarella cheese, then stir until the leaves wilt.

5. Transfer to warmed serving bowls and serve immediately with Parmesan cheese.

KALE PESTO
& SPAGHETTI

SERVES: *4* | **PREP:** *20 mins* | **COOK:** *20 mins*

INGREDIENTS

*225 g/8 oz kale, thick stems and
central ribs trimmed*

40 g/1½ oz pine nuts

450 g/1 lb dried spaghetti

1 large garlic clove

zest of 1 lemon

juice of ½ lemon

125 ml/4 fl oz olive oil

*25 g/1 oz freshly grated Parmesan-
cheese, plus extra to garnish*

*400 g/14 oz canned cannellini
beans*

chia seeds, to garnish

salt (optional)

1. Add a little salt, if using, to a large saucepan of water and bring to the boil. Fill a medium-sized bowl with iced water. Blanch the kale leaves in the boiling water for 45 seconds. Using a slotted spoon, transfer the kale to the iced water. Drain, place in a clean tea towel and squeeze to remove any excess water.

2. Heat a large frying pan over a medium heat, place a layer of baking paper on the base and scatter over the pine nuts. Gently toast until the nuts turn golden. Set aside.

3. Bring the pan of water back to the boil and add the pasta. Cook for 8–10 minutes until tender but still firm to the bite.

4. Meanwhile, combine the kale, pine nuts, garlic and ¾ teaspoon of salt, if using, in a food processor. Add the lemon zest and lemon juice and pulse until smooth. Drizzle in the oil until it is fully incorporated. Add the cheese and pulse to mix.

5. Drain and rinse the beans, then add to the pasta. Immediately drain the pasta, reserving some of the cooking water. Toss the pasta and beans with the pesto. Add a little of the reserved cooking water if needed to coat the pasta nicely. Serve immediately with a generous dusting of cheese and a sprinkling of chia seeds.

TOFU STEAKS WITH FENNEL & ORANGE

SERVES: *4* | **PREP:** *15 mins* | **COOK:** *6–8 mins*

INGREDIENTS

350 g/12 oz extra firm tofu, drained
1 tbsp harissa paste
2 tsp extra virgin olive oil
1 large orange
1 fennel bulb, very thinly sliced
1 small red onion, thinly sliced
8 black olives, stoned and halved
1 tbsp chopped fresh mint, to
  garnish

1. Preheat the grill to high. Place the tofu on a clean tea towel and press lightly to remove any excess moisture.

2. Cut the tofu into four thick triangles. Mix the harissa with the oil. Brush this mixture over the tofu.

3. Lift the tofu steaks onto a baking sheet and cook under the preheated grill for 6–8 minutes, turning once, until golden brown.

4. Meanwhile, use a sharp knife to cut all the rind and white pith from the orange and carefully remove the segments from the membranes, catching the juice in a bowl.

5. Place the orange segments, fennel, onion and olives in a bowl. Mix thoroughly to combine and then divide the mixture between four serving plates.

6. Place the tofu steaks on top, drizzle with the reserved orange juice and garnish with chopped fresh mint to serve.

QUICK & CREAMY FISH GRATIN

SERVES: *4* | **PREP:** *15 mins* | **COOK:** *20–25 mins*

INGREDIENTS

1 tbsp olive oil

2 shallots, finely chopped

150 ml/5 fl oz dry white wine or fish stock

1 bay leaf

200 g/7 oz closed-cup mushrooms, thickly sliced

100 g/3½ oz crème fraîche

500 g/1 lb 2 oz white fish fillets, cut into chunks

175 g/6 oz prawns, cooked and peeled

175 g/6 oz frozen peas

40 g/1½ oz butter

150 g/5½ oz fresh white breadcrumbs

salt and pepper (optional)

chopped fresh parsley, to garnish

1. Heat the oil in an ovenproof saucepan or a shallow, flameproof casserole, add the shallots and fry for 2–3 minutes, stirring occasionally, until soft. Add the wine, bay leaf and mushrooms and simmer for 2 minutes, stirring occasionally.

2. Stir in the crème fraîche and add the fish. Season to taste with salt and pepper, if using. Bring to the boil, cover and simmer for 5–6 minutes until the fish is almost cooked. Preheat the grill to medium.

3. Remove and discard the bay leaf, then add the prawns and peas and bring back to the boil.

4. Meanwhile, melt the butter in a separate saucepan and stir in the breadcrumbs. Spread the breadcrumb mixture evenly over the top of the fish mixture.

5. Place the saucepan under the preheated grill for 3–4 minutes until the topping is golden brown and bubbling.

6. Divide between warmed serving plates, garnish with parsley and serve immediately.

MEDITERRANEAN SOLE
WITH OLIVES & TOMATOES

SERVES: *4* | **PREP:** *15–20 mins* | **COOK:** *20 mins*

INGREDIENTS

1 shallot

1 garlic clove

*1 fennel bulb, fronds reserved to
   garnish*

2 tbsp olive oil

125 g/4½ oz uncooked couscous

*240 g/8¾ oz drained canned
   chopped tomatoes*

*350 ml/12 fl oz vegetable stock
   or water*

*35 g/1¼ oz stoned Kalamata olives,
   chopped*

4 x 175-g/6-oz sole fillets

¼–½ tsp crushed chilli flakes

*1 tbsp fresh oregano leaves or 1 tsp
   dried oregano*

60 g/2¼ oz butter

50 ml/2 fl oz white wine

salt and pepper (optional)

1. Chop the shallot and finely chop the garlic. Trim, core and thinly slice the fennel. Chop the olives. Heat the oil in a large frying pan over a medium–high heat. Add the shallot, garlic and fennel, and cook, stirring occasionally, for about 3 minutes until the vegetables are soft. Add the couscous, tomatoes, stock, olives and 1 teaspoon of salt, if using. Stir to combine.

2. Lay the fish fillets on top of the couscous mixture, in a single layer if possible. Season with salt and pepper, if using. Sprinkle the chilli flakes and oregano over the fish. Cut the butter into small pieces and scatter it over the fish. Drizzle the wine over and around the fish.

3. Cover, reduce the heat to low, and cook for about 15 minutes until the fish is cooked through and the couscous is tender. Serve immediately on warmed plates garnished with fennel fronds.

TUNA NOODLE CASEROLE

SERVES: *4* | **PREP:** *15 mins* | **COOK:** *26–28 mins*

INGREDIENTS

1 tbsp olive oil

1 onion, diced

1 carrot, diced

140 g/5 oz button mushrooms, sliced

450 ml/16 fl oz chicken or vegetable stock

300 ml/10 fl oz canned condensed cream of mushroom soup

475 g/1 lb 1 oz canned tuna in brine

350 g/12 oz dried egg noodles

125 g/4½ oz panko breadcrumbs

55 g/2 oz freshly grated Parmesan cheese

salt and pepper (optional)

1. Preheat the oven to 200°C/400°F/Gas Mark 6. Heat the oil in a large, ovenproof frying pan or wide saucepan. Add the onion and carrot and cook, stirring occasionally. Add the mushrooms to the pan with salt and pepper to taste, if using, and cook, stirring occasionally, for 2–3 minutes until the vegetables begin to soften.

2. Stir in the stock and soup, and bring to the boil. Drain the tuna and add it to the pan, breaking up any big chunks. Add the noodles and stir to coat with the sauce. Cover the pan and transfer to the preheated oven for about 15 minutes until the noodles are tender. Preheat the grill to medium.

3. Remove the pan from the oven and stir the casserole well. Sprinkle the breadcrumbs and cheese evenly over the top, place under the grill for 2–3 minutes until the topping is golden brown and serve.

BEETROOT, LOBSTER & SPINACH RISOTTO

SERVES: *4* | **PREP:** *15 mins* | **COOK:** *30 mins*

INGREDIENTS

*1.5 litres/2¾ pints vegetable or
  chicken stock*
25 g/1 oz butter
2 tbsp olive oil
1 small onion, diced
280 g/10 oz risotto rice
100 ml/3½ fl oz dry white wine
5 small raw beetroots, grated
1 tsp freshly grated horseradish
juice of ½ lemon
175 g/6 oz baby leaf spinach
*225 g/8 oz ready-to-eat lobster
  meat or crabmeat*
*115 g/4 oz freshly grated Parmesan
  cheese*
salt and pepper (optional)

1. Bring the stock to the boil in a large saucepan, then simmer over a low heat. Meanwhile, heat the butter and oil in a separate large saucepan over a medium heat, add the onion and fry for 3 minutes. Add the rice and stir to coat with the butter and oil. Cook for a further 2 minutes. Add the wine and simmer for 2 minutes, or until it has all been absorbed.

2. Add the beetroots and stir well. Add 2 ladles of hot stock to the pan, then cover and cook for 2 minutes, or until absorbed. Stir well and add another ladle of stock. Stir constantly until the stock is absorbed, then add another ladle. Continue adding the stock, one ladle at a time, until it has all been absorbed and the rice is tender but still firm to the bite.

3. Stir in the horseradish and lemon juice, then add the spinach and season to taste with salt and pepper, if using. Divide the risotto between warmed bowls, top with the lobster meat and cheese and serve immediately.

SALMON FILLETS
WITH PESTO

SERVES: *4* | **PREP:** *10 mins* | **COOK:** *10–15 mins*

INGREDIENTS

*4 salmon steaks, about 175 g/6 oz
    each*
*mixed salad and griddled ciabatta,
    to serve*

PARSLEY PESTO

2 garlic cloves, roughly chopped
25 g/1 oz pine nuts
*40 g/1½ oz fresh parsley, coarse
    stems removed*
1 tsp salt
*25 g/1 oz freshly grated Parmesan
    cheese*
*125–150 ml/4–5 fl oz extra virgin
    olive oil*

1. To make the parsley pesto, put the garlic, pine nuts, parsley and salt into a food processor or blender and process to a purée. Add the cheese and blend briefly again. Add 125 ml/4 fl oz oil and blend again. If the consistency is too thick, add the remaining oil and blend again until smooth. Scrape into a bowl and set aside. Preheat the grill to medium.

2. Cook the salmon under the preheated grill for 10–15 minutes, depending on the thickness of the fillets, until the flesh turns pink and flakes easily.

3. Transfer to serving plates, top with the parsley pesto and serve immediately with salad and ciabatta.

CREAMY CHICKEN
WITH PENNE

SERVES: *2* | **PREP:** *10 mins* | **COOK:** *15–20 mins*

INGREDIENTS

200 g/7 oz dried penne

1 tbsp olive oil

2 skinless, boneless chicken breasts

4 tbsp dry white wine

115 g/4 oz frozen peas

5 tbsp double cream

salt (optional)

*4–5 tbsp chopped fresh parsley, to
    garnish*

1. Add a little salt, if using, to a large saucepan of water and bring to the boil. Add the pasta, bring back to the boil and cook for about 8–10 minutes until tender but still firm to the bite. Drain.

2. Meanwhile, heat the oil in a frying pan over a medium heat. Add the chicken and cook, turning once, for 8–10 minutes until the chicken is tender and the juices run clear when a skewer is inserted into the thickest part of the meat.

3. Pour the wine into the pan and cook over a high heat until it has almost evaporated.

4. Add the peas, cream and pasta to the pan and stir well. Cover and simmer for 2 minutes.

5. Transfer to warmed serving plates, garnish with fresh parsley and serve immediately.

CHICKEN & DUMPLINGS

SERVES: *4* | **PREP:** *10 mins* | **COOK:** *25–35 mins*

INGREDIENTS

2 tbsp olive oil

1 large onion, diced

2 celery sticks, diced

2 carrots, diced

1 tbsp fresh thyme leaves

1 tsp salt

½ tsp pepper

4 tbsp butter

60 g/2¼ oz plain flour

2 tbsp milk

1.4 litres/2½ pints chicken stock

1 rotisserie chicken

140 g/5 oz frozen peas

*2 tbsp fresh parsley leaves, finely
chopped, to garnish*

DUMPLINGS

2 tbsp butter

250 g/9 oz plain flour

2 tsp baking powder

¾ tsp salt

225 ml/8 fl oz milk

25 g/1 oz fresh chives

1. Heat the oil in a large, heavy-based saucepan over a medium–high heat. Add the onion, celery and carrots and cook, stirring, for about 3 minutes until the onion is translucent. Add the thyme, salt and pepper, and cook for a further 1 minute. Add the butter and heat until melted, then stir the flour into the butter. Cook until the butter and flour have browned. Stir in the milk and add the stock. Bring to the boil, then reduce the heat to medium and simmer for about 10 minutes. Meanwhile, pull the meat from the chicken carcass and shred it.

2. To make the dumplings, place the butter in a microwave-safe dish. Cover the dish and heat in the microwave on a low setting for 30 seconds, or until melted. Finely snip the chives. Put the flour, baking powder and salt into a bowl and stir to combine. Stir in the butter, milk and chives until just combined.

3. Stir the chicken and peas into the vegetables, then drop small spoonfuls of the dumpling batter on top. Cover and simmer for 12–15 minutes until the dumplings are cooked through. Ladle the casserole and dumplings into bowls. Garnish with the parsley and serve immediately.

MOZZARELLA-STUFFED CHICKEN BREASTS

SERVES: *4* | **PREP:** *15–20 mins* | **COOK:** *15–20 mins*

INGREDIENTS

4 skinless chicken breast fillets

4 tsp ready-made green pesto

125 g/4½ oz mozzarella cheese

4 thin slices Parma ham

250 g/9 oz cherry plum tomatoes, halved

75 ml/2½ fl oz dry white wine or chicken stock

1 tbsp olive oil

salt and pepper (optional)

fresh ciabatta, to serve

1. Preheat the oven to 220°C/425°F/Gas Mark 7. Place the chicken breasts on a board and cut a deep pocket into each with a sharp knife. Place a teaspoon of pesto in each pocket.

2. Cut the cheese into four equal pieces and divide between the chicken breasts, tucking into the pockets.

3. Wrap a slice of ham around each chicken breast to enclose the filling, with the join underneath. Place the chicken in a shallow ovenproof dish and arrange the tomatoes around it. Season with salt and pepper, if using, pour over the wine and drizzle with the oil.

4. Bake in the preheated oven for 15–20 minutes until the chicken is tender and the juices run clear when a skewer is inserted into the thickest part of the meat.

5. Cut the chicken breasts in half diagonally, place on warmed serving plates with the tomatoes and spoon over the juices. Serve with fresh ciabatta.

TURKEY & BARLEY STEW

INGREDIENTS

15 g/½ oz dried ceps

1 onion

450 g/1 lb button mushrooms

4 carrots

2 tbsp olive oil

1 tsp salt

½ tsp pepper

200 g/7 oz barley

600 ml/1 pint vegetable stock,
*   chicken stock or water*

1 tbsp fresh thyme leaves

450 g/1 lb turkey breast meat

55 g/2 oz freshly grated Parmesan
*   cheese*

2 tbsp chopped fresh parsley, to
*   garnish*

1. Place the ceps in a small bowl and cover with hot water. Dice the onion and slice the mushrooms and carrots. Heat the oil in a large saucepan over a medium–high heat. Add the onion and cook, stirring frequently, for 4 minutes, or until soft. Add the mushrooms and carrots to the pan with the salt and pepper. Cook, stirring occasionally, for a further 4 minutes until the vegetables are tender. Add the barley and stir to mix well. Add the stock.

2. Remove the ceps from the soaking water, reserving the soaking liquid, and chop. Add to the pan with the soaking liquid and bring to the boil. Meanwhile, finely chop the thyme and add to the pan. Reduce the heat to low and simmer, uncovered, for about 5 minutes.

3. Meanwhile, cut the turkey into 1-cm/½-inch cubes. Add to the stew, stir to mix, then cover and simmer for 15 minutes until the turkey is cooked through, the barley is tender, and most of the liquid has evaporated. Serve the stew in warmed bowls, garnished with the cheese and parsley.

PORK & APPLE ONE POT

SERVES: *4* | **PREP:** *15 mins* | **COOK:** *30 mins*

INGREDIENTS

25 g/1 oz plain flour
675 g/1 lb 8 oz boneless pork
   shoulder, cubed
2 tbsp vegetable oil
1 onion, diced
4 smoked bacon rashers, diced
2 large green apples, such as
   Granny Smith
350 g/12 oz baby new potatoes
225 g/8 oz green cabbage, shredded
1 tbsp fresh thyme leaves
1 tbsp white wine vinegar
450 ml/16 fl oz chicken stock
225 ml/8 fl oz apple juice
2 tbsp Dijon mustard
salt and pepper (optional)

1. Place the flour in a large polythene bag and season the pork with 1 teaspoon of salt and ½ teaspoon of pepper, if using. Put the meat in the bag with the flour, close the top and shake to coat well.

2. Heat the oil in a large, heavy-based saucepan over a medium–high heat. Add the onion and bacon and cook, stirring, for about 3 minutes until the onion begins to soften and the bacon begins to brown. Add the pork and cook, stirring occasionally, until the meat is brown all over. Transfer the mixture to a bowl. Meanwhile, core and dice the apples and dice the potatoes.

3. Add the apple, potatoes, cabbage and thyme to the pan along with the vinegar, stock and apple juice. Add the mustard, ½ teaspoon of salt and ¼ teaspoon of pepper, if using, bring to the boil, then reduce the heat to a simmer. Return the pork, onion and bacon to the pan and cook, uncovered, for about 15 minutes until the meat is cooked through. Serve immediately.

HAM & LEEK RISOTTO

SERVES: *4* | **PREP:** *10 mins* | **COOK:** *30–35 mins*

INGREDIENTS

380 g/13¼ oz arborio rice

1 litre/1¾ pints water

2 tbsp olive oil

350 g/12 oz cooked ham, diced

1 shallot, diced

2 leeks, white and light green parts
* only, trimmed and diced*

4 tbsp dry white wine

25 g/1 oz finely chopped fresh
* parsley, plus extra to garnish*

1 litre/1¾ pints chicken stock, plus
* extra if needed*

145 g/5¼ oz fresh or frozen peas

25 g/1 oz butter

60 g/2¼ oz freshly grated Parmesan
* cheese, plus extra to garnish*

salt (optional)

1. Rinse the rice under cold running water. Place in a large saucepan with the water and a generous pinch of salt, if using. Bring to the boil over a high heat, then reduce the heat to low and simmer, uncovered, for 7 minutes. Drain in a colander and set aside.

2. Heat the oil in the pan used to cook the rice. Add the ham, shallot and leeks and cook, stirring, for about 3 minutes until the vegetables begin to soften and the ham begins to brown. Add the wine and parsley and cook for a further 1–2 minutes. Add the rice, stock and ¼–½ teaspoon of salt, if using, and bring to the boil. Reduce the heat to medium and simmer, stirring occasionally, for 12 minutes, or until most of the stock has evaporated.

3. Taste the risotto. If it is not yet cooked through, add a little more stock and cook for a few more minutes. Stir in the peas in the last couple of minutes of cooking, then stir in the butter and cheese. Garnish with cheese and parsley and serve immediately.

SPAGHETTI BOLOGNESE

SERVES: *4* | **PREP:** *15 mins* | **COOK:** *30 mins*

INGREDIENTS

2 tbsp olive oil

1 large onion, chopped

500 g/1 lb 2 oz fresh lean beef mince

1 green pepper, deseeded and chopped

1 garlic clove, crushed

150 ml/5 fl oz red wine or beef stock

400 g/14 oz canned chopped plum tomatoes

2 tbsp tomato purée

1 tbsp dried oregano

200 g/7 oz dried spaghetti

salt and pepper (optional)

freshly grated Parmesan cheese, to serve

1. Heat the oil in a large saucepan over a high heat. Add the onion and mince, and fry, stirring, until lightly browned with no remaining traces of pink. Stir in the green pepper and garlic.

2. Add the wine, tomatoes, tomato purée and oregano. Bring to the boil and boil rapidly for 2 minutes. Reduce the heat, cover and simmer for 20 minutes, stirring occasionally.

3. Meanwhile, add a little salt, if using, to a large saucepan of water and bring to the boil. Add the spaghetti, bring back to the boil and cook for about 8–10 minutes until tender but still firm to the bite. Drain the spaghetti in a colander and return to the pan.

4. Season the sauce to taste with salt and pepper, if using, then stir into the spaghetti. Serve immediately with Parmesan cheese.

CLASSIC BURGERS

SERVES: *4* | **PREP:** *15 mins* | **COOK:** *10–12 mins*

INGREDIENTS

750 g/1 lb 10 oz fresh beef mince
1 beef stock cube
1 tbsp finely chopped dried onion
2 tbsp water
2 large tomatoes, peeled, deseeded and chopped
1 tbsp chopped fresh basil
55 g/2 oz Cheddar cheese, grated
fresh basil sprigs, to garnish

TO SERVE

4 burger buns, halved
mustard
tomato ketchup

1. Preheat the grill to medium–high. Place the beef in a large mixing bowl. Crumble the stock cube over the mixture and add the dried onion, water, tomatoes and chopped basil and mix well.

2. Divide the meat into four portions, shape each into a ball, then flatten slightly to make a burger of your preferred thickness.

3. Cook the burgers under the preheated grill for 5–6 minutes. Turn the burgers, sprinkle cheese over the top and cook for a further 5–6 minutes until cooked through.

4. Place the burgers on the bottom halves of the buns and top with the lids. Garnish with sprigs of basil and serve immediately with mustard and tomato ketchup.

MISO STEAK &
PEPPER STIR-FRY

SERVES: *4* | **PREP:** *15 mins, plus marinating* | **COOK:** *15 mins*

INGREDIENTS

350 g/12 oz lean beef steaks
1 tbsp melted coconut oil, for frying
4 spring onions, cut into
 4-cm/1½-inch lengths
2-cm/¾-inch piece fresh ginger,
 peeled and grated
1 carrot, peeled and cut into
 matchsticks
1 red pepper, deseeded and sliced
1 yellow pepper, deseeded and
 sliced
100 g/3½ oz baby corn, halved
1 courgette, cut into matchsticks
100 g/3½ oz mangetout, shredded
1 tbsp soy sauce
2 tbsp sesame seeds, to garnish

MARINADE

2 tbsp brown miso paste
1 tbsp sake
1 tbsp caster sugar
2 garlic cloves, crushed

1. To make the marinade, mix the ingredients together in a non-metallic bowl. Add the steaks and rub all over with the mixture. Cover and chill in the refrigerator until needed.

2. Heat a griddle pan, add the steaks and cook over a medium heat for 2–3 minutes on each side, depending on how pink you like your steak. Remove from the pan and leave to rest.

3. Meanwhile, heat the coconut oil in a wok or large frying pan, add the spring onions and ginger and cook over a medium heat for 2 minutes.

4. Add the carrot, red and yellow peppers and baby corn to the wok and stir-fry for 2 minutes, then add the courgette and mangetout. Stir-fry for a further 3 minutes.

5. Slice the steaks and add to the wok with the soy sauce. Stir-fry for 1 minute until all the vegetables are cooked but not soft.

6. Divide the steak slices and vegetables between four plates and sprinkle with sesame seeds. Serve immediately.

SPEEDY BEEF STEW

INGREDIENTS

900 g/2 lb beef, finely sliced

3 tbsp plain flour

2 tbsp olive oil

1 large onion, diced

2 garlic cloves, finely chopped

225 ml/8 fl oz red wine

450 g/1 lb button mushrooms,
*   quartered*

450 g/1 lb new potatoes, diced

4 carrots, diced

2 celery sticks, diced

700 ml/1¼ pints beef stock

3 tbsp tomato purée

1 tbsp fresh thyme leaves, chopped

2 tbsp chopped fresh parsley

salt and pepper (optional)

crusty bread, to serve

1. Season the beef with ½ teaspoon of salt and ½ teaspoon of pepper, if using. Toss in the flour. Heat the oil in a large, heavy-based saucepan over a medium–high heat. Add the meat and cook, stirring frequently, for about 4 minutes until brown all over. Add the onion and garlic to the pan and cook for 2–3 minutes until the onion begins to soften. Add the wine and bring to the boil, scraping up any sediment from the base of the pan.

2. Add the mushrooms, potatoes, carrots and celery to the pan with 1 teaspoon of salt and ½ teaspoon of pepper, if using, the stock, tomato purée and thyme. Bring to the boil, then reduce the heat to low, cover, and simmer for about 15 minutes until all the vegetables are tender.

3. Remove the lid of the pan and simmer for a further 5 minutes until the sauce is slightly thickened. Stir the parsley into the pan and serve the stew hot, with crusty bread for mopping up the sauce.

MEXICAN BEEF & BEAN BOWL

SERVES: *4* | **PREP:** *10 mins* | **COOK:** *20–25 mins*

INGREDIENTS

1 tbsp olive oil
500 g/1 lb 2 oz fresh beef mince
1 onion, chopped
2 red peppers, deseeded and sliced
2½ tsp chilli powder
400 g/14 oz canned red kidney
  beans, drained and rinsed
400 g/14 oz canned cannellini
  beans, drained and rinsed
400 g/14 oz canned chopped
  tomatoes
1 tbsp tomato purée
100 ml/3½ fl oz vegetable stock
200 g/7 oz basmati rice
2 tbsp chopped fresh coriander
salt and pepper (optional)
soured cream and smoked paprika,
  to serve

1. Heat the oil in a large frying pan, add the mince and cook for 2–3 minutes until brown all over.

2. Add the onion and red peppers and cook, stirring occasionally, for 3–4 minutes.

3. Stir in the chilli powder and cook for 1 minute, then add the kidney beans, cannellini beans, tomatoes, tomato purée and stock. Bring to a simmer and simmer for 12–15 minutes. Season to taste with salt and pepper, if using.

4. Meanwhile, cook the rice according to the packet instructions.

5. Stir the coriander into the chilli and serve in warmed bowls with the rice, topped with a dollop of soured cream and a sprinkling of smoked paprika.

CHAPTER FIVE

DESSERTS & BAKING

HEALTHY COOKIE DOUGH DIP

SERVES: *4* | **PREP:** *8–10 mins* | **COOK:** *No cooking*

INGREDIENTS

400 g/14 oz canned butter beans,
   drained and rinsed
½ tsp bicarbonate of soda
3 drops vanilla extract
2 tbsp almond butter
1 tbsp almond milk
1 tbsp milled linseeds
½ tsp honey, plus extra to taste
50 g/1¾ oz plain chocolate,
   chopped
sliced fresh fruits, such as banana,
   strawberries, pear, mango and
   melon, to serve (optional)

1. Place all the ingredients, except the chocolate, in a food processor and blitz until nearly smooth. Add a little more honey to taste.

2. Stir the chopped chocolate into the dip.

3. Serve with the fruit of your choice, if using.

POACHED RHUBARB
WITH EDIBLE FLOWERS

SERVES: *4* | **PREP:** *10 mins* | **COOK:** *10 mins*

INGREDIENTS

500 g/1 lb 2 oz tender red rhubarb,
*   cut into 7-cm/2¾-inch pieces*
juice of ½ lemon
1¼ tbsp acacia honey or other
*   mild-flavoured clear honey*
100 ml/3½ fl oz hot water
flowers from 3 elderflower heads,
*   rinsed*
2 tbsp edible flowers, such as
*   elderflowers, lavender flowers,*
*   violet flowers and pink rose*
*   petals, to serve*

1. Arrange the rhubarb pieces in a lidded frying pan in a single layer.

2. Combine the lemon juice, honey, water and elderflowers in a large heatproof bowl. Pour this mixture over the rhubarb and bring to a simmer over a medium–low heat. Cover and simmer for 3 minutes, then turn the rhubarb pieces over and simmer for a further 2 minutes, or until it is just tender when pierced with a sharp knife. Using a slotted spoon, transfer the fruit to serving bowls.

3. Stir the liquid to reduce to a syrupy consistency and pass through a sieve to remove the cooked elderflower petals. Spoon the syrup over the rhubarb and decorate with edible flowers to serve.

LEMON POSSET

SERVES: *4* | **PREP:** *15–20 mins* | **COOK:** *No cooking*

INGREDIENTS

*grated rind and juice of 1 large
   lemon*
4 tbsp dry white wine
55 g/2 oz caster sugar
300 ml/10 fl oz double cream
2 egg whites
lemon zest, to decorate
langues de chat biscuits, to serve

1. Place the lemon rind and juice, wine and sugar in a bowl. Mix until the sugar has dissolved. Add the cream and beat with a hand-held electric mixer until it holds soft peaks.

2. Whisk the egg whites in a separate bowl until stiff but not dry. Gently fold into the cream mixture.

3. Spoon the mixture into four serving glasses. Decorate with lemon zest and serve immediately with langues de chat biscuits.

BANOFFEE MERINGUE PIE

SERVES: 8 | **PREP:** 15–20 mins, plus optional cooling | **COOK:** 12–15 mins

INGREDIENTS

1 x 20-cm/8-inch ready-rolled all
   butter round pastry case
400 g/14 oz canned dulce de leche
   (caramel sauce)
1 large banana
3 large egg whites
175 g/6 oz caster sugar
1 tbsp chocolate shavings

1. Preheat the oven to 190°C/375°F/Gas Mark 5. Place the pastry case on a baking sheet. Spoon the dulce de leche into the case and level the surface with a spatula. Peel and thinly slice the banana and arrange the slices on top of the caramel.

2. Put the egg whites into a clean, grease-free bowl and beat with a hand-held electric mixer until they hold stiff peaks. Gradually mix in the sugar, one spoonful at a time, to make a firm and glossy meringue. Spoon the meringue over the bananas and swirl with the back of a spoon.

3. Bake in the preheated oven for 12–15 minutes, or until the meringue is golden brown. Sprinkle the chocolate shavings over the hot meringue and serve immediately or leave to cool.

MINI APPLE CRUMBLES

SERVES: *4* | **PREP:** *15 mins* | **COOK:** *20 mins*

INGREDIENTS

2 large Bramley apples, peeled,
cored and chopped
3 tbsp maple syrup
juice of ½ lemon
½ tsp ground allspice
55 g/2 oz unsalted butter
100 g/3½ oz porridge oats
40 g/1½ oz light muscovado sugar

1. Preheat the oven to 220°C/425°F/Gas Mark 7. Place a baking sheet in the oven to heat. Put the apples into a saucepan and stir in the maple syrup, lemon juice and allspice.

2. Bring to the boil over a high heat, then reduce the heat to medium, cover the pan and cook for 5 minutes, or until almost tender.

3. Meanwhile, melt the butter in a separate saucepan, then remove from the heat and stir in the oats and sugar.

4. Divide the apples between four individual 200-ml/7-fl oz ovenproof dishes. Sprinkle over the oat mixture. Place on the baking sheet in the preheated oven and bake for 10 minutes until lightly browned and bubbling. Serve warm.

STRAWBERRIES & CREAM
FILO TARTS

SERVES: *4* | **PREP:** *25 mins* | **COOK:** *8–10 mins, plus cooling*

INGREDIENTS

25 g/1 oz butter
85 g/3 oz filo pastry
200 g/7 oz strawberries, plus extra
to decorate
2 tbsp strawberry conserve
150 ml/5 fl oz double cream
150 g/5½ oz ready-made custard

1. Preheat the oven to 200°C/400°F/Gas Mark 6. Melt the butter in a small saucepan and use some of it to lightly grease four 10-cm/4-inch tartlet tins. Place the tins on a baking sheet. Use scissors to cut the pastry into sixteen 15-cm/6-inch squares.

2. Stack four squares of pastry on top of each other, each at a slight angle. Brush the top and underside of the stack with the melted butter. Press into one of the prepared tins. Repeat with the remaining pastry and butter to make four cases in total. Bake in the preheated oven for 4–5 minutes, or until golden at the edges. Carefully remove from the tins and gently flip over onto the baking sheet. Bake for a further 2–3 minutes, or until golden all over.

3. Transfer the pastry cases to a wire rack and leave to cool for 12–14 minutes. Meanwhile, hull the strawberries and slice into a bowl, reserving eight whole strawberries to garnish. Stir in the conserve. Whip the cream in a bowl until it holds firm peaks, then fold in the custard. Divide the cream mixture between the pastry cases, top with the strawberries and decorate with a couple of whole strawberries to serve.

CHOCOLATE BAKED ALASKA

SERVES: *6* | **PREP:** *20–25 mins* | **COOK:** *5 mins*

INGREDIENTS

500 g/1 lb 2 oz chocolate ice cream
6 ready-made chocolate brownies
2 large egg whites
115 g/4 oz caster sugar
cocoa powder, for dusting

1. Line a 700-ml/1¼-pint pudding basin with clingfilm. Place the ice cream in the basin. Slice off any excess ice cream above the rim of the basin and cut this into smaller chunks. Push the chunks into the gaps around the main block of ice cream. Top with the chocolate brownies, cutting to fit, if necessary, and press down firmly. Place in the freezer for 15 minutes. Preheat the oven to 220°C/425°F/Gas Mark 7.

2. Meanwhile, put the egg whites into a clean, grease-free bowl and whisk with a hand-held electric mixer until they hold firm peaks. Gradually whisk in the sugar, one spoonful at a time, to make a firm and glossy meringue.

3. Remove the basin from the freezer and turn out onto a baking sheet. Quickly spread the meringue all over the ice cream and the edge of the chocolate brownie base to cover completely. Bake in the preheated oven for 5 minutes, or until the meringue is just set and lightly browned. Serve immediately, lightly dusted with a little cocoa powder.

BUTTERSCOTCH, MANGO & GINGER SUNDAES

SERVES: *4* | **PREP:** *15–20 mins* | **COOK:** *8 mins*

INGREDIENTS

1 large, ripe mango
115 g/4 oz ginger biscuits
1 litre/1¾ pints vanilla ice cream
2 tbsp roughly chopped almonds,
*   toasted*

BUTTERSCOTCH SAUCE

100 g/3½ oz light muscovado sugar
100 g/3½ oz golden syrup
55 g/2 oz unsalted butter
100 ml/3½ fl oz double cream
½ tsp vanilla extract

1. To make the butterscotch sauce, melt the sugar, golden syrup and butter in a small saucepan over a low heat, then simmer for 3 minutes, stirring, until smooth. Stir in the cream and vanilla extract, then remove from the heat.

2. Peel and stone the mango and cut into 1-cm/½-inch cubes. Place the biscuits in a polythene bag and lightly crush with a rolling pin.

3. Divide half the mango between four sundae glasses and top each with a scoop of the ice cream. Spoon over a little of the warm butterscotch sauce and sprinkle with the crushed biscuits. Repeat the layers with the remaining ingredients.

4. Sprinkle the almonds over the top of each sundae and serve.

BANANA FLATBREAD BITES
WITH TAHINI & DATE SYRUP

SERVES: *4* | **PREP:** *15–20 mins* | **COOK:** *5–6 mins*

INGREDIENTS

4 wholemeal tortillas

4 tbsp tahini

4 tbsp date syrup

4 bananas, peeled

1. Preheat a dry frying pan, then add the tortillas, one at a time, and warm for 30 seconds on each side.

2. Arrange the tortillas on a chopping board, thinly spread each with the tahini, then drizzle with the date syrup. Add a whole banana to each tortilla, just a little off-centre, then roll up tightly.

3. Cut each tortilla into thick slices, secure the bites with a cocktail stick and arrange on a plate. Serve warm.

QUICK TIRAMISÙ

SERVES: *4* | **PREP:** *15–20 mins, plus optional chilling* | **COOK:** *No cooking*

INGREDIENTS

225 g/8 oz mascarpone cheese

1 egg, separated

2 tbsp natural yogurt

2 tbsp caster sugar

2 tbsp dark rum

2 tbsp strong, black coffee, cooled to
  room temperature

8 sponge fingers

2 tbsp grated plain chocolate

1. Put the mascarpone cheese, egg yolk and yogurt in a large bowl and beat together until smooth.

2. Whisk the egg white in a separate bowl until stiff, but not dry. Add the sugar and gently fold into the mascarpone mixture. Divide half of the mascarpone mixture between four sundae glasses.

3. Place the rum and coffee in a shallow dish and mix together. Dip the sponge fingers into the rum mixture, break into bite-sized pieces and divide between the glasses.

4. Stir any remaining coffee mixture into the remaining mascarpone mixture and divide between the glasses. Sprinkle with the grated chocolate. Serve immediately, or cover and chill until required.

SUMMER BERRY TARTS

SERVES: *6* | **PREP:** *20–25 mins, plus cooling* | **COOK:** *15 mins*

INGREDIENTS

375 g/13 oz ready-rolled sweet
shortcrust pastry
250 g/9 oz mascarpone cheese
1 tsp vanilla extract
1 tbsp clear honey
400 g/14 oz mixed summer berries,
such as strawberries, raspberries,
redcurrants and blueberries
icing sugar, for dusting

1. Preheat the oven to 200°C/400°F/Gas Mark 6. Unroll the pastry on a work surface and cut into six squares. Place each square in a 10-cm/4-inch loose-based tartlet tin and lightly ease into the tin, without stretching.

2. Roll a rolling pin over the top of the tins to trim the excess pastry. Press the pastry into the fluted sides with your fingers.

3. Place the tins on a baking sheet and prick the pastry with a fork. Line each tin with baking paper and fill with baking beans.

4. Bake in the preheated oven for 10 minutes, then remove the paper and beans and bake for a further 5 minutes. Leave to cool in the tins for 10 minutes. Carefully remove the pastry cases from the tins, transfer to a wire rack and leave to cool completely.

5. Mix the mascarpone cheese with the vanilla extract and honey, then spoon into the tartlets and spread evenly.

6. Halve the strawberries and mix with the remaining fruit, then divide between the tartlets. Dust the tartlets with sifted icing sugar just before serving.

CHOCOLATE & AVOCADO PUDDING POTS

MAKES: *4 pots* | **PREP:** *20 mins* | **COOK:** *5 mins*

INGREDIENTS

*55 g/2 oz plain chocolate, 70%
    cocoa solids, broken into pieces*
*1 large ripe avocado, halved and
    stoned*
4 tbsp canned full-fat coconut milk
4 tsp maple syrup
½ tsp natural vanilla extract
pinch of sea salt

1. Place the chocolate in a bowl set over a saucepan of gently simmering water and heat until melted.

2. Scoop the avocado flesh into a food processor. Process until smooth, then add the coconut milk, maple syrup, vanilla extract and salt. Spoon in the melted chocolate and process until smooth.

3. Spoon the mixture into small shot glasses. Serve immediately or chill in the refrigerator until needed.

LEMON DRIZZLE SQUARES

MAKES: *9 squares* | **PREP:** *20 mins, plus cooling* | **COOK:** *20–25 mins*

INGREDIENTS

115 g/4 oz butter, softened, plus
*   extra for greasing*
115 g/4 oz caster sugar
115 g/4 oz self-raising flour
2 eggs
finely grated rind and juice of ½
*   large lemon*

TOPPING

85 g/3 oz granulated sugar
finely grated rind and juice of ½
*   large lemon*

1. Preheat the oven to 200°C/400°F/Gas Mark 6. Lightly grease a 20-cm/8-inch shallow square cake tin and line the base and sides with baking paper. Put the butter, sugar, flour, eggs, lemon rind and juice into a large bowl and beat with a hand-held electric mixer for 1–2 minutes until pale and creamy.

2. Spoon the mixture into the prepared tin and gently level the surface. Bake in the preheated oven for 20–25 minutes, or until risen, golden and just firm to the touch. Meanwhile, prepare the topping by mixing the sugar and lemon rind and juice together in a small bowl.

3. Remove the cake from the oven and pierce the top all over with a cocktail stick. Spoon the topping over the hot cake. Leave the cake to cool in the tin – the topping will become crunchy as the cake cools. Remove from the tin and cut into squares to serve.

RISE & SHINE
BREAKFAST MUFFINS

MAKES: *12 muffins* | **PREP:** *15 mins* | **COOK:** *25 mins, plus cooling*

INGREDIENTS

125 g/4½ oz plain white flour
75 g/2¾ oz plain wholemeal flour
2 tsp baking powder
½ tsp ground cinnamon
75 g/2¾ oz muscovado sugar
150 g/5½ oz granola
50 g/1¾ oz rolled oats
2 bananas, peeled and mashed
200 g/7 oz Greek-style natural
  yogurt
100 ml/3½ fl oz milk
100 g/3½ oz coconut oil, melted
200 g/7 oz raspberries
1 tbsp pumpkin seeds

1. Preheat the oven to 200°C/400°F/Gas Mark 6. Line the holes in a 12-hole muffin tin with 12-cm/4½-inch squares of baking paper.

2. Put the white flour, wholemeal flour, baking powder, cinnamon, sugar, granola and oats into a large bowl.

3. In a separate bowl, mix the bananas, yogurt, milk and coconut oil together.

4. Pour the wet ingredients into the dry ingredients and lightly mix. Add the raspberries, reserving 12, and mix again; do not over-mix – some flour should still be showing.

5. Divide the mixture between the 12 paper cases, then top each muffin with a raspberry and sprinkle over the pumpkin seeds.

6. Bake in the preheated oven for 25 minutes until golden and risen. Leave to cool in the tin for 5 minutes, then turn out onto a wire rack and leave to cool completely.

FILO PLUM & ALMOND TART

SERVES: *4* | **PREP:** *15 mins, plus cooling* | **COOK:** *21–27 mins*

INGREDIENTS

55 g/2 oz butter, softened

4 x 28-cm/11-inch square filo pastry sheets

5 small red plums

1 egg

55 g/2 oz ground almonds

40 g/1½ oz caster sugar, plus extra for sprinkling

1 tbsp plain flour

custard or cream, to serve (optional)

1. Preheat the oven to 200°C/400°F/Gas Mark 6 and place a baking sheet in the oven to heat up. Melt 15 g/½ oz of the butter in a small saucepan and use some to lightly grease a 20-cm/8-inch round, loose-based tart tin. Brush the filo pastry sheets with the remaining melted butter and layer them in the prepared tin, gently scrunching the pastry around the edge of the tin.

2. Scrunch some foil into a disc and place in the pastry case. Bake in the preheated oven for 4–5 minutes, or until the pastry is just beginning to brown around the edges. Meanwhile, quarter and stone the plums. Put the remaining butter into a bowl with the egg, ground almonds, sugar and flour and beat together until smooth.

3. Remove the foil and spread the almond mixture in the pastry case. Top with the plum quarters and sprinkle with sugar. Return to the oven and bake for 15–20 minutes, or until the pastry is golden brown and the filling is almost set (it will still be wobbly in the middle). Leave to cool in the tin. Serve warm or cold with custard, if using.

BLUEBERRY & LEMON FRIANDS

MAKES: *8 friands* | **PREP:** *20 mins, plus cooling* | **COOK:** *18–22 mins*

INGREDIENTS

*115 g/4 oz unsalted butter, diced,
    plus extra for greasing*
3 large egg whites
pinch of salt
55 g/2 oz plain flour
*150 g/5½ oz icing sugar, plus extra
    for dusting*
85 g/3 oz ground almonds
1 tsp finely grated lemon rind
55 g/2 oz blueberries

1. Preheat the oven to 220°C/425°F/Gas Mark 7. Put the butter into a saucepan and melt over a low heat. Pour into a shallow bowl and leave to cool for a few minutes. Thoroughly grease an 8-hole non-stick muffin tin or friand mould, then place on a baking sheet.

2. Put the egg whites and salt into a large, grease-free bowl and whisk with a hand-held electric mixer for 1–2 minutes until foaming and floppy, but not stiff. Sift in the flour and icing sugar and fold into the egg whites with the ground almonds and lemon rind. Fold in the melted butter to make a smooth batter.

3. Spoon the batter evenly into the prepared mould and scatter over the blueberries. Bake in the preheated oven for 14–18 minutes until risen, golden and just firm to the touch. Leave to cool in the mould for 5 minutes, then turn out onto a wire rack and leave to cool completely. Serve warm or cold, dusted with icing sugar.

GIANT CHOCOLATE CHUNK COOKIES

MAKES: *12 cookies* | **PREP:** *20 mins, plus cooling* | **COOK:** *15–20 mins*

INGREDIENTS

115 g/4 oz butter, softened
125 g/4½ oz caster sugar
125 g/4½ oz soft light brown sugar
2 large eggs, lightly beaten
1 tsp vanilla extract
280 g/10 oz plain flour
1 tsp bicarbonate of soda
300 g/10½ oz milk chocolate,
  broken into pieces

1. Preheat the oven to 180°C/350°F/Gas Mark 4. Line four large baking sheets with baking paper.

2. Place the butter, caster sugar and brown sugar in a large bowl and cream together until pale and fluffy. Beat the eggs and vanilla extract into the mixture until smooth. Stir in the flour and bicarbonate of soda, and beat together until well mixed. Stir in the chocolate.

3. Drop 12 large spoonfuls of the mixture onto the prepared baking sheets, spaced well apart to allow for spreading. Bake in the preheated oven for 15–20 minutes, or until set and golden brown. Leave to cool on the baking sheets for 2 minutes, then transfer the cookies to wire racks and leave to cool.

SUGAR & SPICE
DOUGHNUTS

MAKES: *6 or 12 doughnuts* | **PREP:** *20 mins, plus cooling* | **COOK:** *15 mins*

INGREDIENTS

115 g/4 oz self-raising flour
½ tsp baking powder
70 g/2½ oz caster sugar
1 tsp ground mixed spice
75 ml/2½ fl oz milk
1 egg, beaten
½ tsp vanilla extract
25 g/1 oz butter, melted, plus extra
  for greasing

SUGAR COATING

2 tbsp caster sugar
1 tsp ground mixed spice

1. Preheat the oven to 190°C/375°F/Gas Mark 5. Thoroughly grease a 6-hole doughnut tin or a 12-hole mini muffin tin. Sift together the flour and baking powder into a bowl and stir in the sugar and spice. Make a well in the centre. Mix the milk, egg, vanilla extract and melted butter together and pour into the well. Mix with a wooden spoon until smooth.

2. Spoon the mixture into a piping bag fitted with a plain nozzle (twist the bag around the nozzle before filling to prevent the mixture leaking out, then untwist when ready to pipe). Pipe the mixture as neatly as possible into the prepared tin. Each hole should be about two-thirds full.

3. Bake in the preheated oven for 12–14 minutes, or until risen, golden and firm to the touch. To make the sugar coating, mix the sugar and mixed spice together on a plate. Leave the doughnuts to cool in the tin for 2–3 minutes, then gently ease them out. Toss them in the spiced sugar to coat completely and serve warm or cold.

RASPBERRY & ALMOND CAKE

SERVES: *8* | **PREP:** *20 mins, plus cooling* | **COOK:** *22–25 mins*

INGREDIENTS

115 g/4 oz self-raising flour

¼ tsp baking powder

2 eggs

115 g/4 oz butter, softened, plus extra for greasing

115 g/4 oz caster sugar

40 g/1½ oz ground almonds

175 g/6 oz raspberries

2 tbsp flaked almonds

icing sugar, for dusting

1. Preheat the oven to 200°C/400°F/Gas Mark 6. Place a baking sheet in the oven to heat up. Grease a 23-cm/9-inch round, shallow cake tin and line the base with baking paper.

2. Sift together the flour and baking powder into a large bowl. Add the eggs, butter and sugar and beat with a hand-held electric mixer for 1–2 minutes until pale and creamy. Fold in the ground almonds.

3. Spoon the mixture into the prepared tin. Gently level the surface and scatter over the raspberries and flaked almonds. Bake in the preheated oven for 22–25 minutes, or until risen, golden and firm to the touch.

4. Leave the cake to cool in the tin for 1–2 minutes, then turn out onto a wire rack. Serve warm or cold, dusted with icing sugar.

HOT CHOCOLATE FUDGE LAYER CAKE

SERVES: *8* | **PREP:** *20 mins, plus cooling* | **COOK:** *8–10 mins*

INGREDIENTS

butter, for greasing

3 eggs

*85 g/3 oz caster sugar, plus extra
   for dusting*

85 g/3 oz plain flour

*2 tbsp cocoa powder, plus extra
   for dusting*

200 ml/7 fl oz double cream

*225 g/8 oz ready-made chocolate
   fudge frosting*

*plain and white chocolate curls, to
   decorate*

1. Preheat the oven to 200°C/400°F/Gas Mark 6. Lightly grease a 23 x 33-cm/9 x 13-inch Swiss roll tin and line the base and sides with baking paper. Put the eggs and sugar into a large bowl set over a saucepan of gently simmering water. Whisk with a hand-held electric mixer for 3–4 minutes, or until very thick and pale.

2. Sift in the flour and cocoa powder and gently fold in. Pour into the prepared tin and level the surface. Bake in the preheated oven for 8–10 minutes, or until risen and springy to the touch. Meanwhile, dust a sheet of baking paper with caster sugar and whip the cream until it holds firm peaks.

3. Remove the cake from the oven and turn out onto the prepared baking paper. Cut the cake into three strips horizontally, transfer to a wire rack and leave to cool for 5–8 minutes. Spread the frosting over the top of each strip and sandwich the strips together with the cream. Decorate with chocolate curls and dust with cocoa powder.

INDEX

..... ✕ .....

This edition published by Parragon Books Ltd in 2017
LOVE FOOD is an imprint of Parragon Books Ltd

Parragon Books Ltd
Chartist House
15–17 Trim Street
Bath BA1 1HA, UK
www.parragon.com/lovefood

ISBN 978-1-4748-6891-4

Printed in China

Edited by Fiona Biggs
Cover photography by Al Richardson

The cover shot shows the Moroccan Meatballs with Mint
Yogurt on page 104.

.... *Notes for the Reader* ....

This book uses both metric and imperial measurements.
Follow the same units of measurement throughout;
do not mix metric and imperial. All spoon measurements
are level: teaspoons are assumed to be 5 ml, and tablespoons
are assumed to be 15 ml. Unless otherwise stated, milk
is assumed to be full fat, eggs and individual fruits and
vegetables are medium, pepper is freshly ground black
pepper and salt is table salt. Unless otherwise stated,
all root vegetables should be peeled prior to using.

The times given are an approximate guide only.
Preparation times differ according to the techniques used
by different people and the cooking times may also vary
from those given.